Happy and Glorious

Six Reigns of Royal Photography

With contributions by
Cecil Beaton
Richard Cawston
Frances Dimond
Helmut Gernsheim
Tom Hopkinson
Elizabeth Longford
Roger Taylor

Edited by
Colin Ford

Angus & Robertson · Publishers

NOTE
Numbers in the margins of the text refer to illustrations

Angus & Robertson · Publishers
London · Sydney · Melbourne · Singapore · Manila

This book is copyright.
Apart from any fair dealing for the purposes
of private study, research, criticism or review,
as permitted under the Copyright Act, no part may be
reproduced by any process without written permission.
Enquiries should be addressed to the publisher.

First published by Angus and Robertson (U.K.) Ltd 1977

Designed and produced by
George Rainbird Limited
36 Park Street, London W1Y 4DE

Royal Warrants research by Roger Taylor;
royal films research by Thelma Schaverien;
additional picture research by
Tara Heinemann, Kate Poole and Carol Whitehead.

ISBN 0 207 95744 4

Text set and printed by
Jolly & Barber Ltd, Rugby
Bound by Webb Son & Co. Ltd, London

Contents

The contributors

Sir Cecil Beaton:
photographer, writer, artist;
costume and scenery designer for opera, ballet, theatre and film.
Sir Cecil took the official coronation photograph of the Queen.

Richard Cawston:
documentary film-maker;
Head of Documentary Programmes, BBC Television;
producer and director of the television film *Royal Family*,
and also of the Queen's Christmas Day broadcast since 1970.

Frances Dimond:
Curator of the Photographic Collection
in the Royal Archives, Windsor Castle.

Helmut Gernsheim:
photo-historian, photographer and writer
of numerous historical and biographical books;
author of the definitive *History of Photography*.

Professor Tom Hopkinson:
writer and journalist;
helped to prepare and launch the magazine *Picture Post*,
of which he was Editor 1940–50.

Elizabeth Longford:
well-known biographer and historian;
author of outstanding biographies of
Queen Victoria and the Duke of Wellington;
Trustee of the National Portrait Gallery.

Roger Taylor:
Senior Lecturer in Photographic Studies, Sheffield Polytechnic;
currently working on a biographical study of G. W. Wilson
to be published in 1978.

Colin Ford:
Keeper of Film and Photography, National Portrait Gallery.

Colour plates

Foreword

State portraiture remained the province of the painter until at least the reign of George V, though the Gallery's fine group of *The Royal Family at Buckingham Palace*, painted by Sir John Lavery in 1913, in some sense marks the end of an epoch. The accession of Queen Victoria coincided with the practical and commercial beginnings of photography; but, enthusiasts though she and Prince Albert were for the new medium, the Queen never mistook the needs of monarchy, and for official portraits her favourite painter, Winterhalter, was summoned from Karlsruhe.

Photography was important to Queen Victoria for quite different reasons: it was a technique to be mastered and enjoyed, and a means of recording her surroundings and her family life. As Frances Dimond tells us, she kept a series of portraits of the royal children which eventually ran to forty-four albums and thus provides a fascinating and unique 'illustrated family tree'. How George III, patron of Zoffany and Paul Sandby, would have loved photography! With what zeal and enthusiasm Queen Mary, in more recent times, maintained a detailed photographic record of the daily events in her long and dedicated life as a public figure! But, just as Van Dyck glamorised the Caroline court, so such a record was always mirrored through an accepted ideal of royal conduct in given circumstances. Even today, with the increased informality of the monarchy, and the consequent directness of relationships between photographers and film-makers and members of the royal family – which between them have resulted in many happy and intimate glimpses of royal life – some vestige is bound to survive of the earlier psychological situation, so well described by Tom Hopkinson, when 'every royal personage supplied, or was quickly issued with, his stereotype'. The balance has changed, but reportage and the mystique remain intertwined.

Prince Albert sat for his first photographic portrait in 1842. The illustrations in this book, many of them hitherto unpublished, constitute a magnificent visual survey of six reigns, and most have been specially chosen from the exhibition of royal photographs which the Gallery has mounted to celebrate Her Majesty's Silver Jubilee.

The selection of the photographs for the Jubilee exhibition has been in the hands of my colleague Colin Ford. The design is the work of Richard Buckle. Mr Buckle has nearly reached his own silver jubilee as an exhibition designer; those of us who saw his entrancing *Diaghilev* exhibition of 1954, which marked a revolution in the whole concept of exhibitions, will never forget the experience. We are greatly indebted to him for agreeing to devise *Happy and Glorious*, and can only admire (as we expected to admire) the originality, appropriateness to occasion and inimitable sense of style which have attended its creation. Our warmest thanks go, too, to Joe Pradera and David Dougill, expert assistants in the enterprise.

The Trustees wish to express their deep sense of gratitude to Her Majesty The Queen, who has graciously made available so much material from the Royal Library. They also wish to convey their particular appreciation to Sir Robin Mackworth-Young, the Royal Librarian, and his assistant, Frances Dimond, for their unfailing kindness over many months. They are no less grateful to all those private owners and authorities in charge of public institutions who have helped to make the exhibition possible and, by no means least, to the distinguished contributors to this commemorative book.

JOHN HAYES *Director*
National Portrait Gallery
November 1976

Queen Victoria
1819-1901

Prince Albert
1819-1861

Victoria Adelaide,
Princess Royal
1840-1901

Edward VII
1841-1910

Queen Alexandra
1844-1925

Alice Maud Mary
1843-1878

Alfred, Duke of Edinburgh
1844-1900

Albert Victor, Duke of Clarence
1864-1892

George V
1865-1936

Queen Mary
1867-1953

Louise, Princess Royal
1867-1931

Victoria
1868-1935

Edward VIII
1894-1974

George VI
1895-1952

Queen Elizabeth,
the Queen Mother
1900-

Mary, Princess Royal
1897-1956

Queen Elizabeth II
1926-

Prince Philip
1921-

Princess Margaret
1930-

Prince Charles
born 14 November 1948

Princess Anne
born 15 March 1950

Helena
1846-1923

Louise
1848-1939

Arthur, Duke of Connaught
1850-1942

Leopold, Duke of Albany
1853-1884

Beatrice
1857-1944

Maud, Queen of Norway
1869-1938

Alexander
born and died 1871

Henry,
Duke of Gloucester
1900-1974

George, Duke of Kent
1902-1942

John
1905-1919

Prince Andrew
born 19 February 1960

Prince Edward
born 10 March 1964

From Victoria to Elizabeth

A ROYAL FAMILY TREE

 Monarchs   Consorts

1) The monarchy through six reigns

Elizabeth Longford

Over the last six reigns, the British monarchy has changed impressively, though not out of recognition. Its fundamentals are unalterable. As long as it lasts, it will be constitutional, hereditary, and a focus for national unity. But if Queen Victoria were to return and see how her descendants live now, she would stare in glassy surprise; she might well write in her diary, however, 'We were *much* amused'.

There was a cheerful strain in the early Victorian monarchy despite its legendary gloom. Witness the highly popular paintings of royal babies and doggies. The Queen described one family group, including Prince Albert and his bag of game, as 'very cheerful and pleasing'; so it was, except perhaps for the game. Nor was the monarchy averse to a romantic image. Landseer shrewdly entitled his great stag painting 'The Monarch of the Glen', painting it from *below,* which was found to be the best angle for human monarchs also. Victoria and Albert organised torchlight dances, and, for one fancy-dress ball, dressed up as Queen Philippa and Edward III.

Nevertheless, the legend of a stuffy Victorian monarchy was not totally false. At first it was a reaction against lewdness and licence going back to the Regency. The middle classes welcomed reform and reflected the moral gilding of the Palace in their own moral stucco. But after Prince Albert's untimely death in 1861, the monarchy went into a state of almost pathological withdrawal, emerging at length like an Emperor moth that had been too long in its chrysalis.

Inspired by Disraeli's imperial fantasies, Victoria called herself 'Empress of India'. The mystique of the

7. Victoria and Albert as Queen Philippa and King Edward III, at a fancy-dress ball held in 1842 in aid of the unemployed Spitalfields silk weavers. There were occasions when the Queen was 'not amused', but this was not one of them. Painting by Sir Edwin Landseer.

1–6. *Opposite:* Six monarchs – five crowns
Queen Victoria: small Imperial Crown, huge national veneration
Edward VII: large Imperial Crown, worn with conviction
George V: King-Emperor
Edward VIII: uncrowned King
George VI: Coronation of the last King-Emperor
Queen Elizabeth II: from Coronation to Silver Jubilee, a shining example.

7

8

crown was enhanced by a Queen-Empress decked with oriental gems and possessing a 'Durbar Room' designed by Rudyard Kipling's father. When the European scramble for Africa got under way, Queen Victoria was strongly behind the British people in all their impulses of missionizing, colonisation and aggression. She presented bibles to black chieftains, wept for General Gordon's death, refused to weep over Black Week in the Boer War. She once told a despondent minister 'We are not interested in the possibilities of defeat; they do not exist'.

The years of her married life were now paying dividends. Prince Albert had believed that Europe could be kept at peace through inter-related monarchies. Under his widow's formidable direction, the majority of their nine children married into princely houses. Thus the Victorian monarchy became a dynastic prodigy and its Queen-Empress the great-grandmother of Europe.

Edward VII succeeded to the throne in 1901. He showed a clearer understanding of the constitution than his mother. It was generally believed that a constitutional monarch had the right 'to be consulted, to encourage and to warn'. But Victoria remained convinced that the monarch not only reigned but *ruled*. Rather than operate a 'democratic monarchy', she threatened to abdicate.

The psychological changes in the Edwardian monarchy were equally striking. After Albert died, Victoria became a father to her children instead of a mother, and a Victorian father at that. Her motherly instincts were reserved for her Empire. Edward VII brought up his heir as a friend, and reigned over his subjects as a boon companion. 'Good old Teddy!' they shouted, revelling in the return to pageantry. They seemed to have acquired another 'Merry Monarch'. In fact a new age had begun, the age of mobility. First came the royal motor car, and after that the royal sports car, the Queen's Flight and Prince Philip's helicopter.

163

12

9. Queen Victoria, with her dog Sharp, at Balmoral in 1867.
She ruled her Empire (and her pets) as a mother, and her family as a queen,
but came to prefer the bonnet to the crown.
Photograph by W. & D. Downey.

8. *Opposite:* A mourning family group posed around the bust of the dead Prince Consort, Windsor Castle, 28 March 1862.
From left to right: Princess Alice, Princess Louise, Princess Beatrice,
the Crown Princess of Prussia (Victoria, the Princess Royal), Princess Helena.
Photograph by Bambridge.

10. King Edward VII in his first motor car.
The royal family were to become ever more mobile,
until in the present reign they have been called a 'flying monarchy'.

It was partly through Edward VII's fondness for foreign travel that the monarchy became associated with peace-keeping. Unfortunately his successes in France were counterbalanced by the mutual hostility between himself and his nephew the Kaiser, with whom his son George V was at war four years after he came to the throne in 1910. Of what use were dynastic marriages as peace-makers if they could not even keep the peace between first cousins?

Because of the First World War, George V changed the royal family's name from the German 'Coburg' to something truly British. In 1917 he proclaimed the 'House of Windsor'. The Kaiser remarked maliciously that he was going to see a performance of Shakespeare's *The Merry Wives of Saxe-Coburg-Gotha* No one can doubt that the change, though born of wartime hysteria, strengthened the monarchy.

George V had found his coronation a 'terrible ordeal', and his early life in the navy, coupled with personal shyness, meant that civil ceremonies were as uncongenial to him as they had been relished by his father. At his accession he had been pitchforked into the party violence generated by House of Lords' reform and Irish Home Rule. Asquith, his Liberal Prime Minister, accused the Tories of trying to make the monarchy 'the football of contending parties'.

With the outbreak of war the harassed King was reprieved; his sons were serving officers and he himself played a unifying role. There were moments, indeed, when he became involved in the conflicts between the politicians and the army. But he survived – as he also survived being persuaded by Lloyd George to take the 'King's Pledge' of teetotalism for the duration, as an example to the munition workers. Members of Parliament failed to follow his lead, and Harold Nicolson wrote: 'Mr Lloyd George's crusade has left His Majesty and his Household high and dry'.

On Armistice Day 1918 the King received his reward. He was cheered to the echo when he appeared with his family on the balcony of Buckingham Palace. *The Times* wrote that this exceptional

11. King George V
in 1913, a year of harassment over Irish Home Rule.
The King feared that civil war would break out.
Instead, it was war against Germany, as a result of which
the King changed the name of his royal house
from the German 'Coburg' to the English 'Windsor'.
Photograph by Russell & Sons

12. The Duke of Windsor
had once aimed to introduce a 'modern monarchy'.
His abdication in 1936 put an end to those dreams for the crown,
though he continued to wear his hats at a jaunty angle.
His wistful look as Prince Charming was replaced
by a quizzical expression. Photograph by Dorothy Wilding.

13. A working lad can look at a king.
It was poignant scenes like this one,
during the royal visit of George V to Sunderland in 1918,
which later earned him the title of
'King George the well-beloved'.

ovation was not simply due to his devotion to duty. It was also a tribute to his 'popular sovereignty', which contrasted with Continental autocracy and the many thrones that had crashed.

The post-war age, however, proved disturbing to the sailor-king, with his quarterdeck manner. The twenties rushed into the 'flapper vote', short skirts, bobbed hair and cocktails – not to mention a general strike and two Labour governments. George V's greatest triumph was in making his first working-class ministers feel welcome. His most controversial act was to appoint the Labour Prime Minister, Ramsay MacDonald, as head of a National Government. The King's aim was simply to achieve unity during the crisis of 1931. Constitutionally, it was his prerogative to appoint whom he pleased. But his act split the Labour party, as if by the sovereign's deliberate desire. Hence Sir Stafford Cripps, a Labour

leader, alerted his party to future 'opposition from Buckingham Palace'. Cripps later explained that he meant 'court circles', not the monarch himself, to which the King retorted: 'Who else is there, I should like to know? Does he mean the Footman?'

Despite this episode, another Labour Prime Minister, Lord Attlee, recognised that George V had carried the monarchy forward. He was both a 'rallying point of stability' and a 'focus for the spread of new ideas'. As Prince of Wales, George V's son Edward had planned to create a 'modern monarchy', crossing swords with a courtier who criticised him for being 'too accessible'. The Prince disagreed: 'Times are changing'. But his brief reign as the uncrowned King Edward VIII (from January to December 1936) was too short to accomplish anything notable. As he himself said, his sole innovations were beardless beefeaters and the King's Flight. Yet in one sense his spontaneous personality and up-to-date tastes smoothed the path towards a real 'modern monarchy'. At his best he bridged the generation gap that the First World War had made into a chasm. He was the first royal communicator, speaking for the unemployed: 'Something must be done'.

At the time of his abdication, it was feared that when he spoke on the radio of 'the woman I love', sentimentalists would side with him, the country would be split and the throne would rock or even topple. On the contrary, the country closed ranks behind the new King. Most people agreed that to have for queen a twice-divorced lady with two husbands still living would make a mockery of the monarchy.

Meanwhile, the abdication was, for the ex-King's brother and successor, a very real and agonising event. Fortunately, George VI's idyllic family life with the charismatic Queen Elizabeth and the delightful Princesses Elizabeth and Margaret supported him through the hectic months between his accession and the outbreak of the Second World War. Then, like his father, George VI came into his own. He chose to suffer with his people, declining to move his family overseas, facing the bombing of his palace with stoicism and leaving on record some memorable sayings. In reply to a tribute from a man on a bomb-site – 'Thank God for a good King' – he said: 'Thank God for a good people'. The Queen added: 'I'm glad we've been bombed. It makes me feel I can look the East End in the face'.

Like his father, George VI lived to preside over rapidly changing post-war politics. George V had got on well with Labour ministers, but his son was better still. He could hit it off as king with a critical Labour minister like Herbert Morrison, who found George V 'stiff' though fair, but George VI 'helpful', 'assiduous' and 'friendly'.

Unhappily, the strains of the King's boyhood (he had suffered the tortures of a severe stammer), followed by the abdication and war, took their toll of a sensitive temperament. In moments of depression he felt that the old order was altogether passing away: 'Before long', he once said, 'I shall also have to go'. This was partly ill-health. He died at the early age of fifty-six. His success was to consolidate the monarchy after the abdication, rather than to modernise it. He handed it on, once more much respected because of his own self-sacrificing character, greatly beloved because of his Queen's unique popularity.

Queen Elizabeth, his eldest daughter, was only twenty-six when she succeeded in 1952. She had made a love-match with the brilliant Prince Philip of Greece five years before, and already had a son and daughter, Prince Charles and Princess Anne. Charles was to grow up into an able, talented, unprejudiced and high-spirited Prince of Wales. Anne was to excel at equestrian sports and, like her grandfather, to marry a commoner. In 1959, the Queen had made a significant change in the royal family's name, demonstrating her passionate resolve to maintain a close-knit family unit. She announced that, though the royal house would remain Windsor as before, its family surname would henceforth be Mountbatten-Windsor, Mountbatten being the surname Prince Philip had adopted in 1947.

The moral keynote of the Queen's reign has been the importance of the family to national well-being.

For the first time, royal children have been educated in schools, but, with the cooperation of the Press, sheltered from the glare of abnormal publicity. The Queen and her husband, on the other hand, have made themselves accessible to the public as never before. Informal luncheons and dinners for those who contributed to the arts, professions and business were instituted at the Palace, whereas conventional debutantes' presentation parties were dropped. 'Walk-abouts' showed the Queen treating the people as her family, rather than appearing to them momentarily as a goddess from the clouds. The *Royal Family* film was a true innovation which took the public for the first time inside her palace. Princess Anne's wedding was televised for hundreds of millions of viewers, and one of the prayers during the Queen's Silver Wedding Marriage Service was for 'all the families of this and every land'.

In some respects, to be sure, the Queen's world-wide family has changed. The old Empire disappeared when India became a republic after the Second World War but, with a genius for compromise and brave disregard for logic, the Commonwealth now numbers many republican members, yet acknowledges the Queen as their binding link.

Of the monarchy itself Prince Philip has said characteristically: 'If at any stage people feel it has no further part to play, then for goodness' sake let's end the thing on amicable terms without having a row about it'. Such engaging outspokenness has drawn the sting of captious criticism. Today the vast majority believe that the monarchy (again in Prince Philip's words) 'exists in the interests of the people'. If the royal mystique is less showy, it is more interesting; if the royal prerogative has diminished, what remains is acceptable to all. Accessibility and mobility involve hard work. The Silver Jubilee celebrates the success of a working monarchy.

Queen Victoria used to insist that the sovereign must always look 'earnest' in portraiture, since monarchy was a 'serious' business. Her great-great-granddaughter has developed a new royal life-style. The House of Windsor is both serious and human.

14. Queen Victoria at work in her garden-tent at Frogmore in 1891, attended by her Indian servant.
Her freedom from racial prejudice, though not always appreciated at court,
testified to her feeling for her Eastern peoples. Such was her confidence in them,
that even the sacred despatch boxes were not out of bounds to the 'Munshi'.
Photograph by Hills & Saunders.

15. Armistice Day, 1918:
George V receives an ovation on the balcony of Buckingham Palace at the end of the First World War.
The Press saw in the King a focus for popular joy, unity and the will never to give in.

16. King George VI and Queen Elizabeth inspecting bomb damage in East London during the Second World War.
After Buckingham Palace was hit, the Queen said 'I'm glad we've been bombed.
It makes me feel I can look the East End in the face'.

17. An early 'walk-about'. The Queen pauses to chat to crowds as she walks through Spinningfield, Manchester, in 1971.
'Walk-abouts' were soon to become an essential feature of the monarchy – new style.

19. Queen Elizabeth II at Benares, in India, 1961.
She has never been Queen-Empress, since India, 'the brightest jewel in Queen Victoria's crown', became a republic in 1950,
while still acknowledging Queen Victoria's great-great-granddaughter as 'Head of the Commonwealth'.
The Crown is a personal symbol of association.

18. *Opposite:* The wedding of Princess Elizabeth and the Duke of Edinburgh, in November 1947.
Far from being 'only the husband' (as Prince Albert had complained a hundred years before),
Philip Mountbatten was to be his wife's 'super Chief of Staff',
giving her 'the complete low-down on absolutely anything'.
Photograph by Baron.

20. A remarkable picture of the
entire royal family,
taken at Buckingham Palace
on the occasion of the silver wedding of
Her Majesty Queen Elizabeth II
and Prince Philip in 1972.
Photograph by Patrick Lichfield.

21. The earliest surviving photograph of Queen Victoria, with the Prince of Wales.
Calotype, c.1844–5, probably by Henry Collen, miniature painter to the Queen, and the first professional calotypist.

24

2) Queen Victoria and the new art of photography

Helmut Gernsheim

Queen Victoria came to the throne in 1837, the year in which L.J.M. Daguerre succeeded in taking pictures by the earliest practicable photographic process. The first daguerreotypes imported from France were shown to her on the morning she proposed to Prince Albert (15 October 1839) and the royal couple were to become not only enthusiastic patrons of the art but, as *The Photographic News* of 24 January 1862 acknowledged, good amateurs themselves:

> *As a manipulator in photography the Prince Consort was unsurpassed: in his practice of the art he was greatly assisted by his former librarian, Dr Becker . . . Her Majesty is also a very good photographer. Certainly the art has no reason to complain of want of patronage and support from the Court; so extensive is the collection of negatives which have been taken for and by the members of the Royal family, that it is necessary to have a private printer to keep them and print them when copies are wanted.*

The sixty-four years of Victoria's reign saw the introduction of nearly all the major innovations in photography, which, when she died, was substantially as it is today. Many of the developments – artistic, scientific and technical – began in Britain, owing a great deal to royal encouragement.

At first, the daguerreotype's long exposures made the taking of portraits impossible. But improvements were rapid and in March 1841 Europe's first public portrait studio was opened by Richard Beard on top of the Royal Polytechnic Institution in Regent Street, London. Three months later Antoine Claudet, Daguerre's pupil and first English licensee,

22–23. Early daguerreotypes of Prince Albert, probably taken in March 1842 by William Constable of Brighton.

set up in competition on the roof of the Royal Adelaide Gallery, a few hundred yards from the present National Portrait Gallery.

Several years passed before Queen Victoria sat for her photograph, and then it was not a daguerreotype but a paper photograph or calotype, invented in England by W. H. Fox Talbot. Talbot's first licensee was Henry Collen, miniature painter and drawing master to the Queen, and he opened his studio in August 1841. The earliest surviving photograph of Victoria was almost certainly taken by him in 1844 or 1845. Prince Albert had already been photographed, as the Queen recorded in her diary on 6 March 1842: 'Albert sat yesterday to a man who makes photographic likenesses'. We learn the identity of the photographer from the *Sussex Advertiser* of 14 March 1842:

21

22

23

Mr Constable of the Photographic Institution had the honour of receiving several visits from Prince Albert during the stay of the Court at Brighton and his Royal Highness had several portraits taken.

In April 1847 daguerreotypes were taken of all the royal family:

We both sat in the greenhouse [at Buckingham Palace]*, to Mr Killburn* [sic] *for Daguerotypes* [sic]*, which are not much improved to what they were originally . . . Mine was really very successful. Those of the children are unfortunately entirely failures.*

The children were probably too fidgety, for exposures were still about half a minute. Though these daguerreotypes no longer exist, illustrations 32 and 33 were taken by William Edward Kilburn nearly five years later in one of the hothouses at Windsor Castle. This time the Queen wrote in her journal: 'The day was splendid. Mine was unfortunately horrid, but the children's were pretty.'

Kilburn had opened a studio in Regent Street late in 1846 and was soon counted as one of the country's three leading daguerreotypists. In acknowledgement of his success with the 1847 royal portraits, he was immediately appointed 'Photographist to Her Majesty and His Royal Highness Prince Albert', the first of many to receive this honour (see page 60). Soon afterwards, Nikolaas Henneman, a Dutchman, was appointed 'Her Majesty's photographer on paper'. Originally Fox Talbot's valet, Henneman was set up by his master in a studio in Regent Street, the fashionable address for photographic establishments, in September 1847. His royal appointment came through Talbot's half-sister, the Countess of Mount Edgcumbe, a lady-in-waiting, though there is no evidence that he ever photographed the Queen. Indeed, many of the early royal portraits were taken not by professionals but by Dr Becker and by one of Prince Albert's equerries, Captain Dudley (later Lord) de Ros.

Dr Becker was a founder member of the Photographic Society, of which the Queen and Prince Albert became patrons soon after its formation in 1853. Under his guidance they were initiated into the simple technique of the calotype, and it was also he who introduced them to the founder and first secretary of the Photographic Society, Roger Fenton. Throughout the 1850s, Fenton took many photographs of the royal family and their residences. Early in 1854, he set up a darkroom at Windsor Castle, for his own and royal use. When in May 1853 the Queen and Prince Albert became patrons of the newly formed London Photographic Society, they were said to be 'well skilled and practised in the art of photography' though, unfortunately, none of their photographs seems to have been preserved.

Roger Fenton's expedition to the Crimean War, and the subsequent monumental publication of his war photographs, owed a great deal to royal patronage. In supplying Fenton with letters of introduction to governors and ambassadors on the route and to the commanders in the field, Prince Albert lent all the weight of his position to the undertaking. In consequence Fenton was treated with every consideration and given facilities denied to the famous *Times* correspondent William Howard Russell. On his return to England in July 1855, Fenton was commanded to Osborne for an audience, and a month later the royal couple took about twenty of his Crimean photographs to Paris on their state visit to Napoleon III and the Empress Eugénie.

Napoleon's own contribution to the advance of photography came when he allowed the Paris photographer André Adolphe Disderi to take and publish visiting-card-size portraits of him in May 1859. The carte-de-visite was soon fashionable in France and became equally popular in England when John Jabez Edwin Mayall, seeing Disderi's success, sought permission to take cartes of the royal family, which he did at Buckingham Palace in May and July 1860. 'He is the oddest man I know,' Victoria had commented after her first sitting with him five years earlier, 'but an excellent photographer. He is an American, and a tremendous enthusiast in his work.'

115
24
37
38
39
40

24. Windsor Castle. Photograph by Roger Fenton, 1854.

Hundreds of thousands of Mayall's cartes were sold. Their unparalleled success gave great impetus to every photographer publishing cartes of other celebrities. Soon after the publication of Mayall's *Royal Album* in 1861, it became fashionable to collect cartes, and exchange them, like stamps. At the height of the craze, between three and four million were estimated to have been sold in England annually. One of Victoria's ladies-in-waiting wrote home: 'I have been writing to all the fine ladies in London for their and their husbands' photographs for the Queen. I believe the Queen could be bought and sold, for a photograph.'

More than once the Government contemplated following America's example by adding to the national income with a small tax on each photograph. Gladstone considered a penny tax in 1864 and so did Disraeli four years later, when a penny stamp on each of the five million photographs then sold annually would have brought a substantial contribution towards the cost of the Abyssinian War. Ten years later, when war with Russia seemed likely, the imposition of a stamp duty on photographs once more came under consideration. Such a tax, it was argued, would be to a large extent one on vanity and snobbery, and for fiscal purposes these foibles were regarded as fair game. Each time, however, the idea was dropped – quite possibly on the intervention of Queen Victoria, who on other occasions protested against the imposition of a tax on beer and one on matches on the ground that taxing these simple necessities or pleasures would affect the poorest people most – and carte-de-visite portraits were by that time the poor man's picture gallery.

A firm believer in the multiplication of images by photography, Queen Victoria presented photographs on every possible occasion. Anniversaries in particular were always commemorated by photographs. In 1878, on the 'blessed anniversary' of Prince Albert's birth, Princess Beatrice received an enamel photograph of 'our dear Mausoleum'. Photographs figured prominently on the birthday and Christmas present tables of the royal family and were showered on other relations and on friends. No fewer than twenty copies of the Princess Royal's sixteenth birthday photograph appear on one list in the Queen's handwriting in which she clearly set out whether the recipients – ranging from Prince Albert to Sir Edwin Landseer – should have the photograph penny plain or twopenny coloured, framed or unframed. Gladstone gave vent to his resentment on receiving what he called 'a twopenny-halfpenny scrap' on his retirement, whereas other Prime Ministers had received the Queen's portrait in oil or bronze.

In February 1859, newspapers and popular magazines went into raptures over 'a new triumph in photography' – microphotographs. The Ten Commandments, the Lord's Prayer, a 'mosaic' of all the kings and queens of England, could be reduced to the size of a pinhead 'so exquisitely minute that their beauty and fidelity are discovered only by the use of a powerful microscope'. Queen Victoria, always eager for novelties, had a signet ring made by the inventor of microphotographs, J. B. Dancer. It consisted of five portraits of her family, the whole picture measuring only $\frac{1}{8}$ inch across, magnified by a jewel lens. Soon after Albert's death, Victoria gave some of her ladies gold and drop-pearl pendants containing a tiny photograph 'in remembrance of the best and greatest of Princes, from his broken-hearted widow Victoria R. Dec. 1861'. She herself always wore a bracelet with Albert's enamelled photograph and a lock of his hair, and his portrait was included in many of the published pictures of the widowed Queen.

48

71

76

Cards were affixed to the doors of the Queen's private apartments in the various royal residences, stating that everything within had been chosen and arranged by the Prince Consort. To ensure that no change should ever be made, every object in all the royal private apartments in every royal residence was photographed and catalogued, a procedure which also made possible the exact replacement of worn-out upholstery.

Victoria gave photographic outfits to several of her children (and to foreign royalty). She also arranged professional lessons for them; Prince Alfred learnt the rudiments before going to South Africa in 1860, his parents' intention being that he should have something else to occupy him apart from learning navigation during the long voyages which his naval training obliged him to undertake. In order that he should always have someone at hand to help him, the Queen commissioned Frederick York, a professional photographer, to accompany him. Prince Alfred became an enthusiastic amateur, undertaking all the processing work himself. The Prince of Wales occasionally tried his hand, having been taught by William Ackland and Francis Bedford. Bedford accompanied him on his tour of the East in 1862 and took all the photographs, the Prince confining his interest to a daily enquiry about results, and to taking the occasional exposure after Bedford had prepared the plate and focused the camera.

By 1885, when the Princess of Wales became a keen photographer, technique had been greatly simplified by dry plates. She and her children took lessons at the London Stereoscopic School of Photography, learning to use twin-lens reflex cameras. Royalty regularly attended this school for several years; Queen Victoria's daughters, Princess Helena

25. Queen Victoria, the Prince Consort and the Princess Royal, 25 January 1858.
Daguerreotype by T. R. Williams, taken just before the marriage of the Princess Royal to Prince Frederick William of Prussia.

and Princess Beatrice, were initiated in photographic technique there, as was the Duchess of York (later Queen Mary). Soon they were all happily snapping with their Kodaks, the simplest and most popular cameras for amateurs, presented by George Eastman, their American inventor. In autumn 1897 they participated in an exhibition arranged by the Eastman Company at the New Gallery in Regent Street, side by side with the most celebrated pictorial photographers of the day – Henry Peach Robinson, George Davison, Frederick H. Evans, J. Craig Annan, A. Horsley Hinton. As was to be foreseen, 'the royal pictures claimed the first attention of the fashionable visitors, and they were worthy of more attention than they generally received from photographers. As the first general collection shown by a family which has done much good in the encouragement of photography, they are worth careful study. Naturally, as the royal photographers do not produce their work for exhibition and competition, the pictures generally are interesting on account of their subjects rather than from pictorial quality; but apart from the subjects, many of them are very good work; and some show excellent pictorial quality'. (*The Photogram,* December 1897). The most en-

44 thusiastic and gifted of the royal photographers was
45 undoubtedly Queen Alexandra, some of whose
46 family snapshots were published in *The Graphic* in
47 August 1905 and appeared in book form in 1908.

In the autumn of 1896, J. and F. Downey of South
27 Shields were commanded to Balmoral to photograph the visit of Their Imperial Majesties the Emperor and Empress of Russia. J. Downey was the son of W. Downey, of the more famous London portraitists, and he took with him the firm's new 'Grand Kinematograph camera', only patented by its inventors, T. J. and G. H. Harrison, two months earlier. After taking the still photographs, Downey asked if he might also attempt some moving pictures. Permission having graciously been given, the royal party retired for half an hour to give him time to set up his apparatus. Then, as the Queen wrote in
26 her diary: 'We were all photographed by Downey in

26–27. *Above:* The Emperor and Empress of Russia at Balmoral, 3 October 1896.
Left to right: Francis Clark (gillie), the Duke of Connaught, Tsar Nicholas II,
Princess Patricia of Connaught, Queen Victoria, Princess Helena Victoria of Schleswig-Holstein,
the Tsarina, the Duchess of Connaught, Princess Margaret of Connaught.
Photograph by J. & F. Downey of South Shields. It was on this occasion that Downey took the first
ciné-film (*opposite*) of Queen Victoria and the Tsar.

the new cinematograph process, which makes moving pictures by winding off a reel of films. We were walking up and down, and the children jumping about'. Seven weeks later, after the projection of the film at Windsor by Downey Senior and Junior, she had a better grasp of the idea: 'It is a very wonderful process, representing people, their movements and actions, as if they were alive'. Once again, the Queen was enthusiastically welcoming a new technological advance. But the moving picture camera was soon to cover her funeral: the end of the Victorian age. It was to be another sixty-eight years before the new marvel would reach its peak as a means of recording a reigning monarch and her family 'as if they were alive'.

30
31

This article is a revised and condensed version of a chapter in Helmut and Alison Gernsheim's *Queen Victoria, A Biography in Word and Picture* (London, LONGMANS, GREEN AND CO LTD, 1959)

28. Queen Victoria with her great-grandson, Prince Edward of York (later Edward VIII), July 1897.
Photograph by Hughes & Mullins.

29. *Opposite:* Queen Victoria's funeral procession, 4 February 1901, at Windsor Castle.
Photograph by Russell & Sons, Windsor.

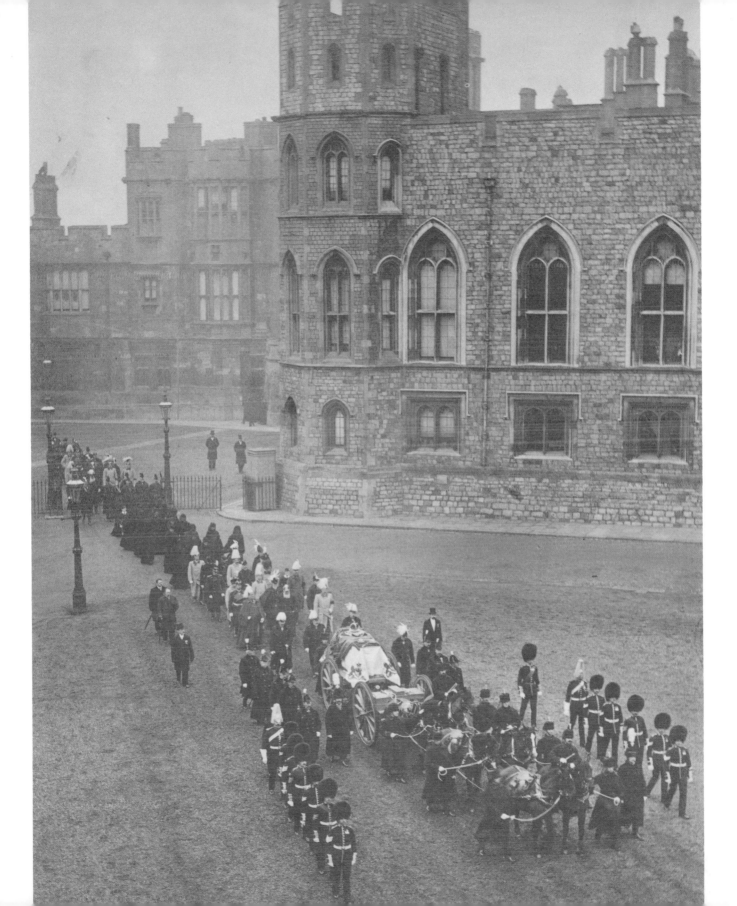

30. A still from one of the films of Queen Victoria's funeral procession, 4 February 1901.

31. Another still from one of the films of Queen Victoria's funeral procession, 4 February 1901.

32–33. Queen Victoria with her five eldest children, photographed by W. E. Kilburn, 17 January 1852. The original daguerreotype (*top*, reversed as daguerreotypes often were) shows (left to right) the Princess Royal, the Prince of Wales, Queen Victoria, Princess Alice, (in front) Princess Helena and Prince Alfred. The Queen's face was presumably erased by Victoria herself; as the carbon copy print (*below*) shows, it was not the most flattering picture of her.

34–36. The royal children performing dramatic extracts from
The Seasons by James Thomson, at Windsor Castle,
10 February 1854, to celebrate their parents' wedding anniversary.
Photographs by Roger Fenton.

37. The cavalry camp at Balaclava. Photograph by Roger Fenton, March 1855.

38. The Council of War: Lord Raglan, Omar Pasha and Marshal Pélissier. Roger Fenton photographed the three allied commanders-in-chief at 5 am on the day of the taking of the Memelon Quarries, 7 June 1855.

39. Lieutenant-General Sir Colin Campbell, photographed by Roger Fenton in the Crimea in 1855.

Disderi.Phot

Déposé

H.R.H. THE PRINCE CONSORT.

40–43. Carte-de-visite photographs: Napoleon III, by Disderi, 1860 (40); the Prince Consort, by J. J. E. Mayall, taken shortly before his death in 1861 (41); Queen Victoria and the Prince Consort, by J. J. E. Mayall, 1 March 1861 (42); Queen Victoria, taken by order of the Queen of Spain at Windsor Castle, 14 November 1861, by Charles Clifford (43).

THE QUEEN & PRINCE CONSORT.

HER MAJESTY THE QUEEN.

Copyright secured. Cundall Downes & Cº 168, New Bond Street.

44–47. Photographs taken by Queen Alexandra during the Norwegian cruise
of the Royal Yacht *Victoria and Albert*, September 1904,
and presented by her to Admiral Rundle.

48. Queen Victoria at the time of her Diamond Jubilee, June 1897.
She wears her wedding veil, and a bracelet containing a miniature photograph of the Prince Consort,
and holds a photograph of the Prince.

THE QUEEN AND H.R.H. THE PRINCESS BEATRICE.

[COPYRIGHT.]

A.J. MELHUISH,   A.J.M.   12 YORK PLACE, PORTMAN SQUARE. W.

49–54. Although few of the countless photographs of Queen Victoria show her smiling, this is partly because the long exposures required by photography during the earlier and happier years of her reign made it difficult to capture the charm of her smile, commented on by those who knew her. 'Those who never saw the Queen's smile can have little idea of the marvellous way in which it brightened and exhilarated the lines of the Queen's features in advancing years. It came very suddenly, in the form of a mild radiance over the whole face, a softening and a raising of the lines of the lips, a flash of kindly light beaming from the eyes'.
(Lady Ponsonby)

55. Balmoral Castle from the north-west, c.1860.
This view shows the castle in all its newness, having been made just a few years after its completion.
The figure seated under the trees is William Gellie, Wilson's assistant for many years.

3) 'The Place and Quality of Photographer to Her Majesty in Scotland'

Roger Taylor

On 8 September 1848, Queen Victoria wrote in her Journal: 'We arrived at Balmoral at a quarter to three. It is a pretty little castle in the old Scottish style. There is a picturesque tower and a garden in front with a high wooded hill.' It must have been a relief to the Queen and her husband to find Balmoral so attractive, for they had taken a lease without seeing it, relying on the water-colours of James Giles for a visual impression, and on their doctor's advice to recommend its dryness and pure air. Its solitude, protected by a tedious and circuitous six-hundred-mile rail journey from London, provided a perfect environment in which to relax from the rigorous formalities of court life, and the purchase of the whole estate was soon negotiated. Immediately Prince Albert set about planning, with his customary enthusiasm, a larger and better arranged castle.

The Royal Burgh of Aberdeen, the third city of Scotland, had been an important town since the twelfth century; its proximity to Balmoral made it a natural source of supply for the Royal Household, and soon a steady stream of expertise, goods and services flowed towards the castle. Among those who were summoned was George Washington Wilson, whose skill as a photographer was to be often in demand.

George Washington Wilson was born on 7 February 1823 on a remote crofting farmstead in north-east Scotland. His father had been a sergeant in the Royal Artillery, served in the Peninsular Wars, lost one wife and three children in a shipwreck and, on returning to his native Scotland, remarried and started another family. George was the second son, educated at the local school and apprenticed from the

56. Chalk self-portrait of George Washington Wilson, aged twenty-six.

57. The symbol used on the reverse of all Wilson's carte-de-visite portraits made at the Crown Street studios until 1873.

45

age of twelve to seventeen to a carpenter and housebuilder.

We do not know what it was that made Wilson take up 'art' but by 1840 he had become a pupil of the Trustees' Academy School of Design in Edinburgh. After Wilson had spent two years as an art student and seven in a teaching post in Aberdeen, his father died and this, coupled with other events, made Wilson decide to spread his wings. He set sail for London, possibly financed by a small bequest from his father. He attended life classes at the Royal Academy, obtained a permit to copy in the National Gallery, and took lessons from a well-established miniaturist and history painter, E. H. Corbould. He even managed a brief excursion to Paris, where he visited other artists' studios and the Louvre.

Back in Aberdeen in late August, he set himself up as a miniature painter and tutor and in December took a wife. During the early years of his marriage, the struggle to establish himself involved several moves of premises, each time westwards towards the better end of town, which eventually brought him to Crown Street in 1852. He subsequently claimed this date as the foundation of his photographic practice, but he had probably already dabbled with the various processes available before that date.

Wilson's work as an artist brought him into contact with the firm of John & James Hay, Carvers and Gilders to the Queen. They must have known of his photographic ability since they approached him in September 1853 to set up a partnership with John Hay junior. In the firm of Wilson & Hay, photographers, Wilson was the photographer and artist, while John Hay provided the frames, the premises and the capital. By December 1853, Wilson and Hay were sufficiently experienced to win both silver and bronze medals in Aberdeen's first photographic exhibition, for 'the general excellence and evidence of progress displayed in their Collodio-Calotype Portraits'.

62 Wilson & Hay's first royal commission was to photograph old Balmoral Castle in 1854 before it was demolished. In March and July of the same year

they recorded the progress of building on the new 61 castle. Their advertisements now included a royal crest, and the words 'Under the Immediate Patronage of Her Majesty'.

Their next commission, in October of the same year, tested Wilson's skill as an artist as well as a photographer. In his photographs of stags shot by 64 Prince Albert, the dead but still noble animal lies at 65 the foot of a tree under the feet of the keeper, the whole arrangement echoing the classical poses of dead and dying heroes surrounded by their faithful followers.

The short-lived partnership of George Washington Wilson and John Hay was dissolved in January 1855. When the royal family returned to Balmoral that autumn, Wilson came to the castle for the first time as an independent photographer and took his first portraits of the Queen and her family.

Prince Frederick William of Prussia had been at Balmoral since 14 September, and on the 20th he spoke to the Queen and Albert of his wish to marry their eldest daughter, the Princess Royal. After some hesitation (she was, after all, only fifteen), they gave their assent; on 29 September the Princess accepted Frederick's proposal. It is not clear exactly when Wilson was asked to the castle, but one suspects he was there for several days before the engagement just so that he could record the actual day. His invoice shows that he was in attendance for thirteen days, 66 but all the photographs which survive are dated 67 29 September 1855.

As a result of his direct contact with the Queen, Wilson now changed his description of himself from 'Under the Immediate Patronage of Her Majesty' to 'Photographer to Her Majesty'. No doubt his new-found status helped his already thriving portrait business in Crown Street.

Wilson was also beginning to emerge as a landscape photographer. Spurred on by successes with stereoscopic views of the Deeside and Aberdeen, he ventured further afield to capture the romantic scenery much loved by the tourist versed in the works of Sir Walter Scott. The Queen's own love of Scott and

58. Mrs Donald Stewart and her children, 1861. One of the series of portraits of the wives of Balmoral keepers and gillies commissioned by Queen Victoria.

59 60. Two pages of a letter from K. Ruland (a member of the Royal Household) relaying Queen Victoria's instructions about the portraits she wished to have taken. See plate above. On the right is a transcript of the complete letter.

Mr. Ruland presents his compliments to Mr. Wilson, and with reference to his intended Photographic Tour to the Highlands in the ensuing Spring, has been directed by Her Majesty to draw Mr. W's attention to the following Views of which she wishes to have Photographs taken:
1 Another view of the Castle of Balmoral itself
1 Birkdale
1 Abergageldie
1 Crathie Kirk
1 East Lodge (near the Bridge)
1 Croft (John Grant's House)
1 West Lodge
1 Rubreck (C. Duncan's House)
1 View of the Village
1 View of Loch Nagar from Larick Chaire (any of the people can show where this is, just above Edmonston's little Shop)
1 Allnaguithnasack
1 The Sheel of the Glassalt
All these views are in the vicinity of Balmoral.
Her Majesty also wishes to have Portraits of the following persons, taken in groups the figures about 3 or 4 – inches in height.
Old Mrs. Grant (John Grant's Mother)
Mrs. Grant, wife of J. Grant & her 2 youngest children

Mrs. Donald Stewart & her children
Mrs. C. Duncan & her children

Mrs. Mackenzie of Allnaguithnasack, and her 2 daughters.

Peter Robertson, James Morgan, Sandy Grant, J. Kennedy, Jennie Smith and Jennie Gine

Buckingham Palace
16th March 1861

P.S.
The Plates of the Portraits must remain private property and therefore Her Majesty will purchase them; with respect to the views near Balmoral Mr. Wilson is at liberty to keep the Plates & sell impressions of them.
Mr. Ruland thinks he has already mentioned to Mr. Wilson the wish Her Majesty expressed to see a photograph of Glen Fishie and Grantown.

47

the Scottish landscape made her an eager customer and she was soon commissioning views that particularly interested her, usually of places she had visited on one of her 'Great Expeditions' into the mountains with Prince Albert. In an 1861 letter she lists a dozen such places as well as asking Wilson to photograph the wives and children of her Balmoral foresters and gillies. The composition of the landscapes she left to Wilson's judgement, but she gave precise instructions that the portraits 'must be in *groups,* the figures three or four inches in height'; advice that Wilson followed carefully.

Two years later, the Queen asked to have her photograph taken in front of a portrait of the now-deceased Albert. To obtain the right mood of quiet dignity as a tribute to his memory, the setting had to be indoors. The room chosen was not designed as a photographic studio and lighting must have posed a considerable problem. Wilson resorted to a conscious optical device that gave strength and force to his picture. By using a large aperture on an uncorrected lens, he produced a whirling centripetal movement around the central figures, who stand out in sharp focus.

The outdoor photographs taken on the same occasion make use of the soft diffused light that is such a feature of the Scottish landscape. One gets the feeling that these were taken very much for the family albums of the English and German royal families. There is a sense of intruding on small intimate scenes rather than looking at formal groupings. The sitters seem at perfect ease with Wilson, and even the very young have been captured with a spark of spon-

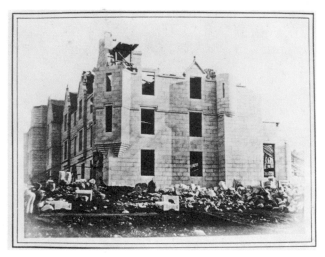

61. The new Balmoral Castle, 1854: one of the sequence of photographs made by Wilson & Hay during the construction of the castle.

62. Old Balmoral Castle, 1854: as it was just before it was demolished and became no more than a commemorative plaque on the lawn.

Opposite: Prince Albert. Hand-tinted daguerreotype by W. E. Kilburn, 1848

HER MAJESTY THE QUEEN.
Copyright reserved Lonsdale Powe & C.º 108 New Bond Street.

taneity that reveals the potential of the 'instantaneous process', a technique that had won him a medal at the 1862 International Exhibition.

Perhaps the most famous portrait of the Queen made by Wilson during this 1863 session was of Her Majesty on the pony 'Fyvie', flanked by John Brown and John Grant. In its original form, this was a memorial to Victoria and Albert's last 'Expedition' on 16 October 1861; later versions were merely portraits of the Queen, or stressed the presence of John Brown when public interest and gossip concerning him and the Queen was at its height.

The Queen's sudden summonses to Balmoral must sometimes have conflicted with Wilson's burgeoning career as a landscape photographer. In July 1865, *The British Journal of Photography* noted:

Mr. Wilson, while pursuing his congenial photographic occupation in securing maritime views at our English seaports, has been honoured with the Royal command to proceed to Balmoral, where Her Majesty is at present sojourning. Like a true loyal subject our friend of the camera has relinquished – at least for the time being – a brilliant summer campaign in obedience to the Royal behest; and no doubt, during the present brilliant weather, Mr. Wilson is carrying out with his usual zeal the commands of his Sovereign. We trust that this inimitable artist will still be able, before the conclusion of the season, to resume again his nomadic wanderings southwards and accomplish even yet much of the artistic work left unfinished when Her Majesty commanded his presence at her Highland residence.

But there were compensations: in 1864, Wilson's firm recorded a total sale of photographs of the royal

63. Monaltrie cottage, Crathie, c.1873.

family with 12,716 prints, which had a value of £500 (a sum worth at least twenty times as much today).

The only photographic evidence of Wilson's 1865 dash northwards is a group of portraits of the Princes Arthur and Leopold in settings that are unusually contrived. They fall uncomfortably between two styles, being neither studio nor outdoor photographs. This compromise was probably the result of a change in the Queen's attitude. She no longer wanted Wilson's inspired family portraits, with their strong flavour of Balmoral, but seemed to prefer the ambiguous anonymity of a grey screen and a rather rumpled carpet.

George Washington Wilson it seems, must have occupied a very special place as one of Queen Victoria's tradesmen, no doubt helped by his long-standing friendship with John Brown, whose influence with the Queen is well known. But his own warmth, geniality and openness of character were exactly the qualities most admired and respected by the Queen. On 17 July 1873, as if to show her gratitude for nineteen years of loyal service, she appointed Wilson to 'The Place and Quality of Photographer to Her Majesty in Scotland'. On a more personal level, and in a gesture which he probably appreciated more, she allowed a cottage on the Balmoral estate to be used by the Wilson family as a summer residence.

64. A group of keepers with the stag shot by Prince Albert on 5 October 1854.

65. Keeper Macdonald with the stag shot by Prince Albert on 5 October 1854.
This photograph was later used as the basis of a line illustration by Queen Victoria in her popular
Leaves from the Journal of our Life in the Highlands 1848–1868.

66. Prince Frederick William of Prussia, 29 September 1855. An informal portrait taken in the grounds of Balmoral on the day of his engagement to the Princess Royal.

67. A family group showing the royal family with Prince Frederick William of Prussia, 29 September 1855. All the photographs taken on the day of the engagement were hastily printed by Wilson and were ready for the Queen to despatch on 4 November, along with her letter to Frederick's father in Germany informing him of the engagement.

68. Prince Frederick William, who had become Crown Prince of Prussia, with his son Prince William, who later became Kaiser. Balmoral, October 1863.

69. Portrait of George Washington Wilson, c.1855.

70. Portrait of George Washington Wilson, taken in his own studio during the 1860s.

71. Queen Victoria with Princess Alice and Princess Louise, Balmoral, October 1863.

72. Queen Victoria with her granddaughter, Princess Victoria.

73–75. Queen Victoria on her pony 'Fyvie',
flanked by John Brown and John Grant,
Balmoral, 1863.
Opposite is the original version as commissioned
by the Queen and entitled in her own album
'A Highland Widow'.
In the second version (*left*)
Wilson vignettes Brown into anonymity
and loses Grant altogether,
focusing the picture on the Queen
rather than on her attendants.
The final version (*above*)
was published by Marion & Co,
when public interest in
Queen Victoria
and John Brown was at its peak.

76. The Prince Consort's room at Balmoral, *c*.1866, taken by Wilson.

77. Queen Victoria's bedroom at Balmoral, *c*.1866, taken by Wilson.

78. Queen Victoria at Balmoral, May 1868, with the Prince of Wales,
the Princes Arthur and Leopold, the Princesses Louise and Beatrice and guests,
including the Duchess of Athol (the left-hand figure on the steps).
Photograph by Downey.

79. Queen Victoria with some of her family in the tent specially erected
for the Gillies' Ball at Balmoral, May 1868.
Photograph by Downey.

Royal Warrant Holders During Queen Victoria's Reign

'Photographer to the Queen', 'Under Royal Patronage', 'Photographer Royal', 'By Special Appointment to Her Majesty'. After the introduction of the popular carte-de-visite to Britain in the early 1860s, portrait studios multiplied rapidly and, from their widespread use of such phrases, one might well have the impression that a large proportion of them had among their regular clientele British and foreign royalty, or at least distinguished members of the nobility. That is exactly what the studio owners wanted a status-hungry public to think. But photographers, like other nineteenth-century businessmen faced with a fierce competition for customers, were able to advertise their wares unhampered by such inhibiting restrictions as today's Trade Descriptions Act. Even the frequent use of the royal standard, and of crests and coats of arms, to hint subtly at royal connections, went virtually unchecked until the passing in 1880 of the Merchandise Marks Act, which at last gave the Lord Chamberlain a measure of control and redress against misuse.

In fact, only those businesses issued with warrants by the Lord Chamberlain's office could properly claim that they were 'By Appointment' to Her Majesty. As the following chronological list shows, no more than 47 of these were given to photographers throughout Victoria's long reign. Many notable names do not appear, even some – such as J. J. E. Mayall – who often photographed the Queen and members of her immediate family (some of whom could, of course, issue their own warrants). But a royal warrant was not a mark of quality, nor even necessarily of special favour. It simply acknowledged that the monarch had regularly ordered, and paid for, goods or services from its holder over a period of at least three consecutive years.

James Ross and John Thompson,
Photographers at Edinburgh to Her Majesty
14th June 1849

Antoine Claudet,
Stereoscopic photographist to Her Majesty
9th July 1855

Mr. Adolfe Disderi,
Photographer in Ordinary
12th March 1867

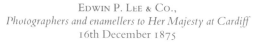

Robert Hills *and* John Henry Saunders,
Photographers
27th April 1867

Mr. Robert White Thrupp,
Photographer to Her Majesty at Birmingham
9th October 1867

Mr. James Valentine,
Photographer to Her Majesty at Dundee in Ordinary.
Personal warrant not extending to future members of the firm
28th November 1868

G. W. Wilson,
Photographer to Her Majesty in Scotland
17th July 1873

EDWIN P. LEE & CO.,
Photographers and enamellers to Her Majesty at Cardiff
16th December 1875

William *and* Daniel Downey,
Photographers in Ordinary to Her Majesty
24th March 1879

Signor C. Macozzi,
Photographer to Her Majesty in Ordinary at Milan
14th December 1880

Mr. John Thompson,
Photographer to Her Majesty
11th May 1881

Mons. Eugene Degard,
Photographer to Her Majesty at Nice.
This warrant is strictly personal
26th June 1882

Mr. Alexander Laurant Henderson,
277 Lewisham High Road, S.E. *London,*
Photographic enameller to Her Majesty
21st November 1884

HUGHES AND MULLINS,
Photographers to Her Majesty at Ryde
15th January 1885

Mr. Thomas Heinrick Voight,
Photographer to Her Majesty at Hamburg
7th February 1885

Messrs. Pierre Louis Pierson, Paul Gaston Braun,
and Jean Jacques Leon Clement,
trading as A. BRAUN AND CO.,
Photographers to Her Majesty at Dornach and Paris
19th March 1885

Herr Karl Backofen,
Photographer to Her Majesty at Darmstadt
31st March 1885

John Collier,
Photographer to Her Majesty at Birmingham
14th October 1885

Stanislas Julien, Comte Ostorof
trading as VALERY, *Photographer to Her Majesty*
19th April 1886

Richard Brown *and* Joseph Bell
trading as BROWN, BAINES AND BELL,
Photographers to Her Majesty at Liverpool
1st July 1886

Messrs. George Taylor *and* Andrew Taylor
trading as A. & G. TAYLOR,
Photographers to Her Majesty
26th October 1886

James Lafayette,
Photographer to Her Majesty at Dublin
5th March 1887

Mr. Charles Albert Wilson,
Photographer to Her Majesty in Scotland
4th May 1887

Mr. George Piner Cartland,
Photographer to Her Majesty at Windsor
2nd August 1887

Cavaliere Carlo Brogi,
Photographer to Her Majesty at Florence
12th May 1888

Messrs. Robert Annan, John Annan, James Craig
Annan *and* Alexander MacKendrick,
trading as J & R. ANNAN & SONS,
*Photographers and photographic engravers to Her Majesty
at Glasgow*
26th September 1889

Edward Lettsome, John Lettsome, Edward W.
Lettsome *and* Allen Lettsome,
trading as LETTSOME & SONS,
Photographers to Her Majesty at Llangollen
12th February 1890

William *and* Daniel Downey,
Photographers to Her Majesty
7th June 1890

Alexander Bassano,
Photographer to Her Majesty
24th November 1890

Mons. F. Burin,
Photographer to Her Majesty at Grasse
29th June 1891

MESSRS. REYA DEEN DAYAL & SONS,
Photographers to Her Majesty at Bombay and Secunderabad
19th September 1891

M. P. Poullan Fils,
Artistic photographer to Her Majesty at Hyères
4th July 1892

Mr. Frederick Saunders *and* Mr. Ernest Saunders
trading as HILLS AND SAUNDERS,
Photographers to Her Majesty at Eton
16th March 1893

Mr. Charles Albert Wilson, John Hay Wilson *and*
Louis Wilson
trading as G. W. WILSON & CO.,
Photographers to Her Majesty in Scotland
6th February 1895

LONDON STEREOSCOPIC AND PHOTOGRAPHIC COMPANY,
Photographers to Her Majesty
7th August 1895

Mr. Robert Milne,
Photographer to Her Majesty at Ballater
28th January 1896

Mrs. Mary Steen,
Photographer to Her Majesty at Copenhagen
21st May 1896

Mr. Horatio Nelson King,
Architectural photographer to Her Majesty
25th August 1896

Charles James Gunn *and* William Slade Stuart
trading as GUNN AND STUART,
Photographers to Her Majesty
24th September 1896

Mr. Thomas Fall,
Photographer to Her Majesty
29th January 1897

Professor E. Uhlenhuth,
Photographer to Her Majesty
5th March 1897

Mr. William Oldham,
Photographer to Her Majesty at Eton
3rd April 1897

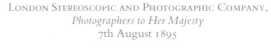

John Lennon Russell, A. Hewing Russell *and* Edward
George Russell
trading as RUSSELL & SONS,
Photographers to Her Majesty
3rd May 1897

William H. Grove,
Photographer to Her Majesty
21st November 1899

Mr. R. Welch,
Photographer to Her Majesty at Belfast
1st June 1900

Mr. W. Abernethy,
Photographer to Her Majesty at Belfast
1st June 1900

Messrs. Herbert Fox *and* Fred Glover
trading as MAULL & FOX,
Photographers to Her Majesty
5th September 1900

80. Queen Victoria with her daughter Princess Beatrice and son-in-law, Prince Henry of Battenberg, and their children, Prince Alexander (in kilt), Princess Victoria Eugénie and Prince Leopold (baby), November 1889. Photograph by Watson.

4) Some royal family albums

Frances Dimond

Members of the royal family have been interested in photography since the early stages of its development, and a number of their albums are now in the Royal Collection. They show aspects of life common to most people – the family, work, holidays, special occasions and ordinary pursuits – but they are particularly appealing because they relate to royalty, and reveal their owners, apparently so well known, in an unexpected light. The following selection is from the albums of the five principal collectors.

'Portraits of Royal Children', a series of forty-four uniformly bound albums, identified and dated in copper-plate writing, might have served as a useful reminder to Queen Victoria of her many descendants. It covers the years 1848 to 1899, and most of the individuals who could claim her as an ancestress are depicted. Some of the royal children shown in the early albums had become grandparents by the last volume, but their portraits were still included, and it is fascinating to see how their appearance changed. The albums not only provide an illustrated family tree, but also give a very good idea of fashions, hair styles, the way people posed for photographs, their interests and occupations.

Although the series covers half a century, the records of successive royal children are remarkably similar, perhaps because they were all brought up during the Queen's lifetime, and often under her influence. They were constantly portrayed in Highland dress, or sailor suits, playing musical instruments or, when very young, riding in panniers on the back of a donkey or pony. Fancy-dress balls and tableaux vivants were popular diversions, and it was usual to have portraits taken on important occasions, such as birthdays and confirmations, and on promotion in the Army or Navy. The custom of dressing sisters or brothers alike is amply demonstrated.

Queen Victoria herself is rarely seen in the early albums, even during the life of the Prince Consort, but she appears more often from the late 1860s onwards: with her family in 'four generations' groups, with parties of descendants at Osborne or Balmoral, and at weddings. Her presence emphasises the idea of a family, the chief impression the albums convey.

Queen Victoria's third son, Arthur, Duke of Connaught, lived to be over ninety, and spent most of his long life in military and official duties. Much of his photograph collection concentrates on public activities – ceremonial occasions, manoeuvres, reviews, inspections, and visits to Ireland, India, South and East Africa. Three volumes recording his time in Canada as Governor-General from 1911–16 contain postcards, newspaper cuttings and photographs, labelled by his younger daughter, Princess Patricia. The Duke's long involvement with the Army is illustrated not only by many photographs of him at the military functions which he attended until the end of his life, but also by the collection of pictures of the 1850s to 1880s which he kept in a book of 'Military Photographs'. The Crimean War is included, as well as groups of soldiers off duty, like the Royal Engineers' Football Club. Prince Arthur himself appears in regimental groups and with officers.

In contrast, there are some family albums, generally arranged by the Duchess of Connaught, containing many circular snapshots made with one of

81. Prince Arthur (left) and Prince Alfred wearing Sikh Indian dress, Osborne, 6 September 1854. Photograph by Dr E. Becker.

82. Princess Alice (standing), Princess Helena and Princess Louise (seated), Osborne, July 1858. Photograph by Captain Dudley de Ros.

83. Group, September 1882, showing how sisters or brothers were dressed alike,
and including the Prince and Princess of Wales, their two sons and three daughters,
the Grand Duke of Hesse, his son and four daughters,
Prince and Princess Christian of Schleswig-Holstein and their two sons.

84. Prince William of Prussia, later Emperor William II
of Germany, at Windsor, 28 November 1863.
Photograph by Hills & Saunders.

85. Princess Margaret of Connaught, January 1886.
Photograph by Mullins.

the Kodak cameras presented to the royal family by their inventor, George Eastman. One of these prints shows the Duke encouraging his daughters to swim at Osborne, in 1893. There are also pictures of house-parties attended by the Duke and his family, sometimes with the signatures of guests on the opposite page.

89

88

93

86. Victoria, Princess Royal, later Empress Frederick of Germany, August 1855. Photograph by J. J. E. Mayall.

87. *Right:* Victoria, Empress Frederick, with her grandson, Prince George of Greece, June 1891.

88. *Below left:* The Duke of Connaught encourages his daughters, Princesses Margaret and Patricia, to swim in the bathing-machine, Osborne, August 1893.

89. *Below right:* A Kodak No. 2 camera, 1889, as used for the picture left.

Opposite
The Four Generations: Queen Victoria, with the Prince of Wales and the Duke of York (later George V), holds Prince Edward of York (later Edward VIII and Duke of Windsor). Photograph by W. & D. Downey, 16 July 1894; hand-coloured print made in 1934 for presentation to the Prince of Wales.

*Four Generations—Queen Victoria, King Edward VII.
(When Prince of Wales) King George V (When Duke of York)
and Prince Edward in the arms of his Great-Grandmother*

90. Officers of B Battery, 4th Brigade, Woolwich, March 1869. Prince Arthur is seated on top of the gun, and Lieutenant Arthur Pickard is on his left, behind the gun.

91. The Royal Engineers' Football Club, Chatham, *c.* mid 1860s.

Left: King George V making his first Christmas broadcast, from Sandringham, 1934.

92. The Duke of Connaught listening to the Band of the Grenadier Guards at Cannes, Easter 1933. Photograph by E. H. Caron.

93. Group at Bessborough, 1909. Front row, left to right:
Princess Patricia of Connaught, Countess of Bessborough, Duke of Connaught, Earl of Bessborough, Duchess of Connaught.
Members of Lord Bessborough's family are also present, including Viscount Duncannon and Lady Gweneth Ponsonby
who are standing on the right.

Queen Alexandra never forgot her Danish background, and although devoted to her family and homes in England, returned almost annually to Denmark for family reunions, and paid frequent visits to her brother, King George I of the Hellenes. These visits were sometimes combined with Northern or Mediterranean cruises of which the Queen, being a good sailor, was fond. As Helmut Gernsheim has pointed out, she was an enthusiastic photographer and kept albums containing many of her own pictures, as well as commercial views, postcards and small water-colours. In the spaces between the illustrations, she described the cruise in a lively narrative.

In 1893, the future Queen Alexandra, then Princess of Wales, went on a Norwegian cruise with her daughters, Princesses Victoria and Maud. Their portraits appear on the first page of an album, with pictures of their dogs and a list of their suite. There is a map of the route and a view of Sheerness, 'the last of dear England'. Many other photographs have descriptive titles: 'This is the bridge we crossed', 'The way we pass our time on deck', 'Myself basking in the sun with dogs'. During a Mediterranean cruise in 1899, Princess Maud, who was unusually slender, was photographed in Corfu with a peasant woman of ordinary size 'to show the difference in *waists*!'.

Queen Alexandra kept similar albums commemorating state visits paid by King Edward VII and herself, and there is an interesting contrast between two of these: the 1908 visit to Reval, on the Baltic Sea, and the 1909 visit to Berlin. At Reval, the King and Queen met the Russian Imperial Family, and the obviously happy occasion is illustrated with many informal pictures, decorative menus, music programmes and postcards. Relations with the German Imperial Family, however, were less easy. Queen Alexandra's narrative, written around the formal photographs, describes an unfortunate mishap which occurred while she was riding in 'a gorgeous yellow State carriage' with the German Empress and her daughter. The uncooperative behaviour of the horses compelled them to change vehicles: 'So out we bundled, Empress and all'.

94. Maud, Princess Charles of Denmark, with a peasant woman in Corfu, 1899.

95. Queen Louise of Denmark with members of her family on her 81st birthday, 7 September 1898.

96. A page from Alexandra, Princess of Wales's album of the Norwegian cruise, 1893.

97. Postcard, with portraits of the German and British sovereigns, commemorating
the visit of King Edward VII and Queen Alexandra to Berlin in 1909.

98. Carlos being washed, during a Mediterranean cruise in 1899.

100. Emperor Nicholas II
and Empress Alexandra Feodorovna of
Russia, Reval, June, 1908.

99. Queen Alexandra making an excursion
to the top of the Rock of Gibraltar
on a donkey, 30 March 1905

101. *Opposite:*
A page from one of Princess Victoria's albums.
In the top row are George, Duke of York,
Grand Duchess Olga Nicholaevna of Russia and
Prince Henry of Battenberg.
The little girl with the bricks is
Princess Nina Georgievna of Russia.

Princess Victoria, the second daughter of King Edward VII and Queen Alexandra, never married and so spent much of her time with her parents, especially her mother, until the Queen's death in 1925. Although she took part in public duties, her life was more private than that of many members of the royal family, particularly as her health was often poor. But she enjoyed taking and collecting photographs, possessing a large number of albums dating from the 1880s to the 1930s. These are nearly all filled with closely arranged snapshots of herself, her relatives and friends, and their activities. Some are in chronological order, others have a haphazard collection of pictures taken at different times, jumbled together like a patchwork screen. A favourite trick was to cut out the figures from one print and glue them on to another, perhaps populating a previously uninhabited room. Similarly, a lady dressed as Cleopatra for a fancy-dress ball has been joined by Prince Francis of Teck in a fez.

Princess Victoria's sense of fun is evident throughout her collection: she enjoys a joke with her grandfather, King Christian IX of Denmark; her poodle Sam balances precariously on the backs of two chairs; and her cousin, Princess Marie of Greece, glares into the camera with fiercely folded arms. Princess Victoria also liked to photograph the rooms which she used in her parents' various homes, in the friends' houses where she stayed, and in the hotels and boarding houses in resorts where she was obliged to go for her health. Perhaps this was because she had to wait so long for a house that was really her own.

102. Princess Victoria in her room at Balmoral, March 1908.

103. Princess Victoria of Wales (right) and her cousin, Princess Marie of Greece, on board H.M.S. *Crescent*, 1898.

104. Queen Alexandra at the entrance of her house
on Snettisham Beach, March 1911.

105. The room used by Princess Victoria at Park Place,
Harrogate, 1915.

106. Group at Trafford Park, October 1887. The party includes Princess Victoria Mary of Teck
(back row, wearing a light-coloured costume) and her parents, the Duke
(back row, left) and the Duchess of Teck (front row, 4th left, wearing a striped costume).

77

107. The Delhi Durbar, 12 December 1911.

The impression gained from Queen Mary's photograph albums is of someone constantly occupied. The thirty-three large volumes, bound in red leather and cloth, date from 1880 to 1952, and give a more complete biography than the other collections. Up to the last volume, the Queen labelled all the photographs herself, sometimes adding explanations later if she thought them necessary; it is clear that, although the albums were personal, they were also intended as a record for posterity. The early volumes are calm and leisurely, with few photographs on each page, but after Queen Mary's marriage in 1893, and particularly after King George V's accession to the throne in 1910, they multiply rapidly, with increasing public duties and social functions. The Coronation, the Delhi Durbar, the Silver Jubilee, as well as visits abroad, and to hospitals, factories, and the troops, are all recorded, as are many family occasions.

In the early volumes, Queen Mary, as Princess Victoria Mary of Teck, appears at home at White Lodge, and abroad, with her parents and brothers; later at Frogmore or Balmoral, with her husband and children. There are photographs illustrating her interest in antiques, gardens, houses and places of historical importance, as well as her visits to theatres and exhibitions. In contrast to the many dignified portraits, there are informal ones showing her digging potatoes at Windsor during the First World War, and enjoying 'wooding' at Badminton during the Second. On reaching the final album the feeling of knowing Queen Mary well is so strong that it is easy to regret parting from her.

107

109

109. *Opposite:* Queen Mary shopping in Edinburgh, with Sir Derek Keppel in attendance, August 1924.

108. Queen Mary, with Princess Beatrice (left) and Princess Mary (right), receiving gifts for sailors and soldiers, on behalf of Queen Mary's Needlework Guild, at Friary Court, St James's Palace, 8 June 1917.

W. & D. DOWNEY.   57 & 61, Ebúry Street, London.

THE PRINCESSES VICTORIA AND MAUD OF WALES.

111. The Princesses Elizabeth and Margaret.
Photograph by Dorothy Wilding.

110. *Opposite:* The Princesses Victoria and Maud of Wales as bridesmaids
at the wedding of their sister, Princess Louise, and the Duke of Fife, 27 July 1889.

5) The official portrait

Cecil Beaton

It was at the end of the fourteenth century that artists began to paint the kings and queens of England. Before that, royal images were enshrined only in effigies and sculptures, and on coins. Fashionable artists from many countries were summoned by succeeding English monarchs to perpetuate their likenesses – Holbein, Van Dyck, Zoffany, Lely, Winterhalter. 'King', 'queen', 'prince', 'princess' – the very words are magically evocative of centuries of history. Understandably these men tended to idealise their subjects.

Then in the early part of the nineteenth century, after the exciting discoveries of Daguerre and Fox Talbot, came the advent of photography and, naturally enough, royal personages allowed themselves to be subjected to this new invention. Now came the opportunity of seeing exactly what the Queen and her family really looked like. The very first photograph of Queen Victoria, with the Prince of Wales, was taken about 1844, probably by Henry Collen (see page 24). Camille Silvy photographed many members of the royal family, but not Victoria her-

114. *Opposite:* A page from the daybooks of Camille Silvy, showing four carte-de-visite photographs of Princess Alice, taken on 4 July 1861, when the Princess was eighteen.

112–113. Carte-de-visite photographs of Prince Albert (*left*) and the Prince of Wales, taken by Camille Silvy on 3 July and 20 June respectively, 1861.

H.R.H.ᵗ 4745 A

The Princess Alice

1861

H.R.Hᵗ 4746 B

The Princess Alice

H.R.H. 4747 C

The Princess Alice

H.R.Hᵗ 4748 D

The Princess Alice

115. Queen Victoria and Prince Albert, photographed at Buckingham Palace by Roger Fenton, 30 June 1854.

self; the natural freedom of the poses he created reminds one of the paintings of Gainsborough. Roger Fenton was commissioned by the Queen to record intimate domestic scenes of the royal family, 115 and his large prints were received with awe and wonder (see opposite). Subsequently many other photographers followed suit, each with their own individual style. If one compares a portrait of Queen 116 Victoria by Franz Winterhalter in 1855 with a 117 contemporary photograph of her taken by J. J. E. Mayall the striking difference between the reality and the ideal is plainly seen.

Great human interest was contained in all the photographs of Queen Victoria and her family, par- 122 ticularly the one of her with the Prince of Wales, the Duke of York, and Prince Edward of York taken by Downey at White Lodge, Richmond Park, after the 118 christening of the young Prince. Edward VII was photographed on all and every occasion, officially and unofficially, from the time of his birth: as an undergraduate at Oxford, on his many travels, at his wedding, with his children, with his dog Caesar, and on his death-bed.

By all standards, early Victorian photographs can be considered works of art. For composition, portrayal of character, and general atmosphere of reality they have never been bettered. It is true that the patina of time is very flattering. We notice the quaintness and charm of a stilted gesture or pose. Old albums have a quality of great period charm; but it is only the best which assumes a timelessness.

The noble and distinguished work of Victorian photographers gave way to commercial flattery and artificiality. The real people who were the subjects of early daguerreotypes were replaced by Edwardian figures stiffly standing to attention with every line and shadow erased from their faces. Downey brought a certain humanity to his work, but his pictures were too heavily retouched, except for those 124 that he took of Queen Alexandra, which still conveyed much of that lovely lady's oval shaped face and porcelain complexion.

Under the awesome glitter and the privilege kings

116–117. Queen Victoria in 1855: a water-colour by Winterhalter (*below*) and a photograph by J. J. E. Mayall, taken at Osborne House. It is instructive to note the contrast between the painter's gentle idealism and the direct truthfulness of the camera.

118

120

121

119

W. & D. DOWNEY
PHOTOGRAPHERS
57 & 61, EBURY STREET,
LONDON, S.W.
COPYRIGHT

122

2451 Z   THE LATE KING EDWARD VII.   ROTARY PHOTO. E.C.
WITH HIS FAVOURITE DOG CÆSAR.

123

118–123. Edward VII – a much photographed king: 118. the scholar at Oxford, c.1860 (photographed by Hills & Saunders); 119. the leader of fashion (J. J. E. Mayall, 1868); 120. the family man, with the Princess of Wales, Prince Albert Victor, Prince George, Princess Louise and the baby Princess Victoria (W. & D. Downey, 1868); 121. the man about town ('Nadar'); 122. the grandfather, with Queen Victoria, the Duke of York, later George V, and Prince Edward of York, later Edward VIII and Duke of Windsor (W. & D. Downey, 1894); 123. the country gentleman, with his favourite dog, Caesar (T. H. Voight).

124. Queen Alexandra on her coronation day, August 1902.
Photograph by W. & D. Downey.

125. King George V in the uniform of the Royal Horse Guards.
'. . . a poignant grandeur that could not be approached with intimacy'.
Photograph by Bassano.

and queens are human, and have the same feelings and emotions as the rest of us; despite discipline and protocol, the personality and character of a ruler will make its mark. The camera reveals and records these qualities, which cannot be hidden from the eye of the lens. Somehow King George V and Queen Mary 125 had personalities which set a distance between them and their public. It was not coldness, rather a poignant grandeur that could not be approached with intimacy. An early photograph by Lafayette of 126 Queen Mary (when she was Duchess of York), stiffly corseted, impassive and expressionless, emphasises this remoteness. Significant was Queen Mary's diffidence about smiling, and the off-hand way in which she acknowledged the cheers of the multitude with a staccato nod of the head and a gauche movement of the gloved hand. People understood and accepted this reticence, sympathising with a Queen who could not allow herself the abandon of lesser subjects, and they loved her right to the end.

To his portraits of royalty, Marcus Adams brought an informality and spontaneity that was new. He recreated the romantic atmosphere of the great portrait painters of the eighteenth and early nineteenth centuries, Raeburn, Romney, and Lawrence. His pictures of the Duchess of York and her child- 129 ren against a tapestry background were delightful. However, his colleague Bertram Park found that 127 although he enjoyed the honour of photographing 128 the British royal family, the hard and fast rules set by the Palace were outdated and irksome.

Queen Elizabeth, the Queen Mother, introduced a warmer, more melting sympathy when responding to the plaudits of the crowd. It is her special ability to be touching and wistful with a simple beautiful grace, to use gestures that are really unhurried. Her Majesty moves in slow motion; her acknowledging hands are precisely employed. I took my first formal photographs of her in 1939. There are certain people who are photogenic and others who are not, and I suspected that Her Majesty belonged to the latter. I knew I would have to use all my experience and ingenuity. I considered that, of all painters, the most

126. An early photograph of Queen Mary by Lafayette.

127. Queen Elizabeth when Duchess of York.
Photograph by Bertram Park.

128. King George VI when Duke of York.
Photograph by Bertram Park.

129. Queen Elizabeth when Duchess of York, with the Princesses Elizabeth and Margaret.
Photograph by Marcus Adams, 1936.
'Marcus Adams . . . recreated the romantic atmosphere of the great portrait painters of
the eighteenth and early nineteenth centuries . . .'

131. Queen Elizabeth, wearing a spangled white tulle dress
and diamond tiara, in the Blue Drawing Room
at Buckingham Palace, 1939.
Photograph by Cecil Beaton.

132. Queen Elizabeth in the garden of Buckingham Palace, 1939.
She wears a champagne-coloured garden-party dress
and picture hat, and carries a parasol,
the handle of which belonged to Catherine of Russia.
Photograph by Cecil Beaton.

130. *Opposite:* Queen Elizabeth, wearing a black velvet crinoline,
and diamond necklace and tiara,
in the Music Room at Buckingham Palace, 1948.
Photograph by Cecil Beaton.

133. Princess Elizabeth,
wearing the Grenadier Guards badge on her cap, 1942.
Photograph by Cecil Beaton.

134. *Opposite:* Her Majesty the Queen
in the robes of the Most Noble Order of the Garter.
Photograph by Cecil Beaton.

suitable to express the Queen's personality would have been Renoir; that his palette could best portray the opalescent delicacies of her complexion and sympathetic warmth of the thrush-like eyes. But my job was with the camera and that is a relentless, impersonal medium. In the soft summer light coming through the Palace windows the Queen looked lovely. I was afraid that perhaps when artificial light was added the effect might not be delicate enough, but when the lamps, placed low on the Savonnerie carpets, went on in a blaze, the Queen looked even more radiant. How could I fail to make entrancing pictures? I was later to take pictures of Her Majesty that were in contrast to any that had been taken before; against a painted background she was wearing a black velvet crinoline with tiara and diamonds like robins' eggs around her throat. I also took photographs for official purposes of King George VI in the uniform of the Royal Air Force.

131

130

My earliest pictures of the present Queen were taken at Buckingham Palace when she was a schoolchild of tender age dressed in a long pink silk dress fashioned in the Gainsborough style. During the Second World War, I photographed the two sisters many times on different occasions – when, wearing tweed and the kilt, they and the King and Queen entertained Mrs Roosevelt at the Palace, and later, when Princess Elizabeth wore the military cap and badge of the Grenadier Guards.

During one long, cold, war winter, I was summoned to Windsor Castle. The State Rooms were magnificently ornate with yellow or red brocaded walls, huge portraits and marble busts, and everywhere a wealth of gilt; the tremendously tall doors did not seem to keep out the draughts. The cold was so intense that one's breath came out in clouds of white mist. Yet when the young Elizabeth appeared on the Gothic landing to be photographed in a fairy-story-like setting, she wore only the lightest of summer clothes.

The Princess was very agreeable and comported herself through a long day's photography with tact, patience, and a certain subdued gaiety. She had al-

ready acquired the same hesitance of speech and the gift for the *mot juste* as her mother, though when the Queen was present her eldest daughter made little conversational effort.

When the birth of a son and heir to Princess Elizabeth and the Duke of Edinburgh was announced, the world waited expectantly for the first photograph of the child who might one day be king. The proud mother, with wild-rose complexion, periwinkle-blue eyes, and a cool refreshing smile, came in wearing a slate-blue dress, followed by a nurse holding the precious bundle. Bows left and right. My assistants were presented in turn; and an awed silence descended as we all, electricians, assistants and property boys alike, took our first look at the baby whose large blue eyes surveyed the world about him with such wonder. I was fascinated by the looks of surprise, disdain, defiance, anger, and delight that ran across his tiny face.

Some remarkable portraits of Prince Charles and Princess Anne were taken by Lord Snowdon. Norman Parkinson was responsible for the excellent pictures of Prince Charles taken at the time of his investiture at Caernarvon Castle; and his photographs of Princess Anne on her twenty-first birthday were beautiful.

It may be a truism, but the Queen is much better looking in life than in any of her photographs. Her complexion always surprises one by its incandescence; her smile has always an unexpected radiance. She is benevolent; her regard is gentle and unhurried, filled with human understanding and kindness. She is meek but not shy; assured and even proud. It is probably true that she exerts a far greater influence on public consciousness than the first Elizabeth. The Duke of Windsor once observed that, when he was a boy, he and his brothers often passed unrecognised during their holidays on the Isle of Wight. Today newsreels and newspapers, feature articles and books, make the Sovereign and her family constant and familiar figures to millions of subjects at home and in the farthest corners of the world. Their images are engraved in the mind and heart of the nation. They constitute an endless source of interest.

135

135. First picture of Prince Charles, with his mother, Princess Elizabeth, 1948. Photograph by Cecil Beaton.

6) Royalty and the newspaper photographer

Tom Hopkinson

The press lives by clichés, even today. Shop stewards must be trouble-makers; landowners reactionary; dockers and stockbrokers hearty, and every Arab an 'oil-rich sheikh'. Forty years ago, when Edward VIII came briefly to the throne, most of the press had no use for anything except clichés, and 'a good Fleet Street man' meant one who had learned the appropriate stereotype for any situation.

If daily life had to be reported in terms of the appropriate cliché, how much more was this true of royalty, the very soul and centre of tradition? Every royal personage supplied, or was quickly issued with, his stereotype: Edward VII, worldly and self-indulgent, but wise, far-seeing and dignified; George V, no intellectual, but going to the heart of the matter with manly simplicity; and Edward VIII, landed from his earliest public appearance with the horrifying label of 'Prince Charming'.

To the photographer of that era, the clichés were guide rules to success, and a knowledge of them as essential as the ability to handle his ponderous Speed-Graphic or Speed-Graflex camera. A newspaper photographer was not expected to think, or 'worry about fancy angles', but to bring back a sharp, well-focused version of 'the picture'. 'What's the picture?' a cameraman would ask his picture editor on leaving for an assignment – or a friend from another paper if he arrived on the scene late. There was seldom any doubt. Everyone was after the same shot: Edward VII in his carriage bowling smoothly to Epsom or Ascot; George V on the moors with his gun raised, or at the helm of his yacht; the Prince of Wales, hesitant, smiling, dressed with a desperate elegance

as though the clothes would somehow see the job through. The cameraman's concern was simply to ensure that his version of the stereotype came across sharp and complete, the personage unobscured by detectives, umbrellas or common citizens, and then to rush it to the office. Since this was all that was asked, his status (like his pay) was low, about on the level of a clerk or petty officer, and much below that of his writing colleagues.

After establishing some rapport with the visiting politician or film star, a journalist would ask 'Do you mind if I bring in my photographer?', rather as though this were some ungainly dog liable to shake himself all over the furniture. And the photographer, having secured 'the picture', usually a toothy likeness, smiling and precise, would vanish as rapidly as the waiter delivering a tray of drinks.

However, the royal stereotype was not only a newspaper convention; it was firmly implanted in the minds of some of the royal personages, remaining there long after photography itself had undergone radical change. Towards the end of the war, when there was talk of King George of Greece going back to Athens to resume his throne, I arranged to take a cameraman to visit him in Claridge's where he was living. It had been explained that this was to be an interview with informal pictures which would accompany and illustrate the text as though the King himself was talking to the readers. But when we arrived at the hotel we found that the King had firmly in his mind what he felt was an appropriate royal pose. He was ready to take this up as many times as necessary, standing always with military

136. *Opposite:* Royalty and the press cameras. The technical advances of the thirties led to a new, more immediate and more natural style of press photography, yet as late as 1937 press photographers were expected to remain at a considerable distance from their subject. King George VI arrives in Launceston during his tour of Devon and Cornwall in December 1937.

137. The Fleet Street 'Prince Charming' stereotype:
the Prince of Wales during his Canadian tour, 1919.

138. A new style of press photography:
the Duke of Windsor, photographed through the window of his car,
leaving Windsor Castle for Portsmouth after making his
abdication broadcast, December 1936.

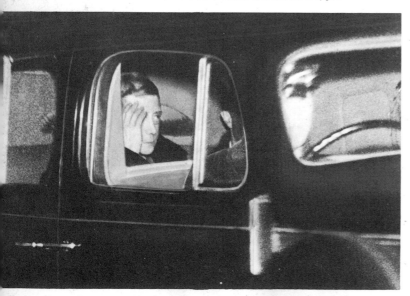

erectness and a truly regal absence of expression, but not to vary it in any way. After efforts to induce some relaxation, we were obliged to give up the attempt.

This was in contrast to the attitude of King George VI, when we got permission in December 1944 to photograph him with his famous postage stamp collection. He had already met the cameraman, Kurt Hutton, on an earlier assignment; chatted with him on arrival, cooperated readily over the arrangements, and soon became absorbed in talking about the stamps. Kurt Hutton had no stereotype for the King, and it appeared that he had none about himself. The resulting pictures were pleasant and informal.

The transformation of press photography, which eventually came to affect 'royal' pictures as well as others, began in the 1930s and, like everything else in the newspaper business, took effect extremely slowly. It started in Germany with the invention of a camera, the Ermanox, followed by a whole range of improvements in an already existing miniature camera, the Leica. These made possible a completely new kind of photography: cameras were smaller and less conspicuous; they could function by 'available light', so that pictures could be taken indoors without flash; and, using the 35mm film developed for the cinema, they allowed far more pictures to be taken at much greater speeds. The posed shot now became a sequence, taken often without the subject's knowledge, and, as the new possibilities showed themselves, the old stereotypes started to crack up.

Sharpness was no longer all important. Revelation was what mattered – conflict, the flash of humour, some fresh variation in the infinite capacity for expression of the human face; what the picture conveyed, not what it showed; its emotional force more than its obvious statement. First exploited in German

Opposite
Queen Elizabeth II and Prince Philip with Charles, Prince of Wales, and Princess Anne in the grounds of Buckingham Palace, 10 October 1957. Photograph by Lord Snowdon.

magazines of the late twenties and early thirties by a photographer of genius, Dr Erich Salomon, 'candid' photography might have remained there much longer but for Adolf Hitler. His activities brought to Britain two notable exponents of the new technique, Felix H. Man and Kurt Hutton, whose work was first seen in a small magazine, *Weekly Illustrated,* and later in *Picture Post* under its first editor, Stefan Lorant.

The new style of photography affected even the most rigid of stereotypes, those of royalty, and the change produced can be strikingly seen in two newspaper pictures taken before and after it occurred – 137   'Prince Charming' signing the book on his Canadian visit of 1919, and Edward VIII in 1936, seen through 138   the window of his car as he vanishes into abdication and obscurity It is not just the tragic change of situation; it is a transformation of the way that such a change in situation could be shown. Before the 'candid camera' revolution, the abdication picture could never, I believe, have appeared. It was too haunting and revealing, too directly in conflict with the royal stereotype. Picture editors would have turned it down for 'lack of quality' (*i.e.* sharpness). Editors would have thrown it out as 'in bad taste'.

By 1938 Fleet Street had so far been affected by the change that for the coronation of George VI, the *Daily Express* arranged to make use of the pictures taken by one of the greatest exponents of the modern outlook, Henri Cartier-Bresson. To their amazement, Cartier-Bresson turned in no 'coronation' pictures at all. What interested him were not the royal party in their playing-card outfits, but the crowd – a man fallen asleep among old newspapers and rubbish 139   after too long a wait; an old lady hoisted up on to strong shoulders to catch a glimpse of the procession. So far from taking stereotypes, Cartier-Bresson had not even photographed the subject – he had found his own. What he was looking for was not 'the picture', but *a* picture.

Opposite: Charles, Prince of Wales, on his 24th birthday, 14 November 1972, with his cousin Lady Sarah Armstrong-Jones, at Balmoral. Photograph by Patrick Lichfield.

139. One of the pictures taken by Henry Cartier-Bresson for the *Daily Express* at the coronation of George VI, 1937. 'So far from taking stereotypes, Cartier-Bresson had not even photographed the subject – he had found his own'.

For me the difference is summed up in a talk I had many years ago with the 'father of the candid camera', Dr Salomon. I was praising his historic picture of   140   'The Two Prime Ministers', Ramsay MacDonald and Stanley Baldwin, and asked how, when every photographer in Fleet Street must have been present on that occasion – the first press conference of the new National Government in 1931 – he alone secured the shot.

140. 'The Two Prime Ministers':
Stanley Baldwin and Ramsay MacDonald photographed by Erich Salomon,
'the father of the candid camera',
at the first press conference of the National Government, 1931.

'I had gone to the Foreign Office', he explained, 'with all the other photographers. Baldwin and MacDonald posed a few times, the others took their pictures and went away. But I had not yet seen any picture, so I stayed. I had my camera on a tripod, ready focused, with a long lead in my hand. They were talking, and I sat there – half an hour, one hour – but still I had not seen any picture. Then the two stopped talking and a journalist at the back of the room asked a question. The two old men leaned forward with their hands to their ears. I saw a picture, pressed the button, got up and went away.'

That was nearly half a century ago. So what is the position today? In the various competitions held annually for 'Photographer of the Year' and similar awards, one of the categories in which newspaper and agency men submit their work is still, as it has always been, 'Royalty'. And what is being looked for, I have thought on these occasions, is a typically British compromise: a picture with some freshness of outlook, some liveliness of incident, some humour of expression – but it is also expected to manifest, or at any rate not conflict with, an underlying stereotype in which the Queen must always be charming; Prince Philip humorously incisive; and Prince Charles always a buoyant extrovert.

So perhaps the great photographic revolution, like most other revolutions, has not taken us very far.

141. Learning the royal salute. The Prince of Wales driving to Kensington with Queen Mary in 1911.

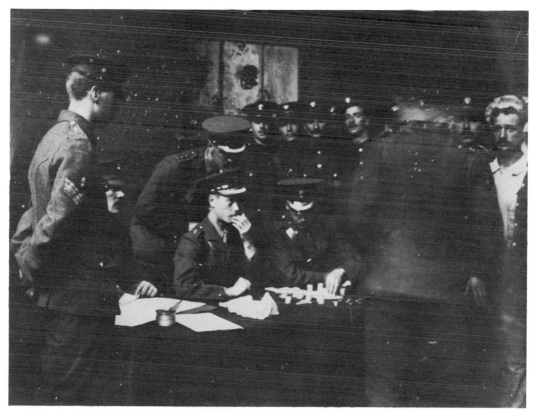

142. A favourite photograph of the Prince of Wales acting as Paymaster to the Grenadier Guards in 1914.

143. A photograph 'prepared' for printing: the photograph seen by a newspaper's readers was not always quite as originally taken by the photographer. The Prince of Wales being greeted by Lord Ebbisham on his arrival for the Advertising Club Dinner at Grosvenor House, 6 July 1934.

144. 'Something must be done'. The Prince of Wales visits the poor and unemployed in the Rhondda Valley, 1932.

145. The first press picture of the Prince of Wales and Mrs Simpson together, taken secretly by James Jarché with a miniature camera in 1935.

146. The first official pictures of the Duke of Windsor and Mrs Simpson, taken at the Château de Candé, 7 May 1937.

148. The Prince of Wales as 'Chief Morning Star',
the title given him by the Stony Creek Indians in Alberta
during his Canadian tour, 1919.

147. *Opposite:* The Prince of Wales and Prince Albert (later King George VI) visiting Lloyd's, 1919;
'. . . dressed with a desperate elegance, as though the clothes would somehow see the job through'.

149. The Prince of Wales,
talking to General Sir Harry Rawlinson,
during an inspection of the Royal Fusiliers
at Bordon Camp, Hampshire.

150. A ducking for the Prince of Wales while riding at a point-to-point.
He was ordered by King George V to give up steeplechasing,
after a series of bad falls.

151–152. 'The servant of the Empire'. The Prince of Wales at Aden, November 1921 (*above*), and at a palaver of chiefs at Accra during his African tour, 1925.

153. The Prince of Wales tiger shooting in Nepal.
Gandhi called for a boycott of the Prince's tour, but many were captivated by his charm and sincerity.

154. An outstanding 'candid' press photograph:
the Duke and Duchess of Windsor at Berchtesgaden, visiting Hitler, 1937.

155–156. Relaxed photography:
King George VI with his postage stamps.
From *Picture Post*, 23 December 1944.
Photographs by Kurt Hutton.

157. A 'stolen picture',
of the Duke of Windsor and Sir Walter Monckton
watching the rehearsal of the
Trooping the Colour, 1952.

158. The Prince of Wales faces the cameras in a film studio,
for the making of the Gaumont British film *The Prince of Wales*, 1932.

7) The royal family on film

Richard Cawston

A film-maker is obviously not the right person to attempt to assess the historical significance of any film he has made – that is better left to historians and critics. What can be said here, as a straight fact, is that nothing like the television documentary *Royal Family,* involving such total and frank participation by the monarchy, had ever been done before nor has been done since – whether in still photography, film, television, radio or even journalism. Among all the media it remains unique, and the credit for this rests firmly within Buckingham Palace, from where the original concept came.

The background to this initiative can be explained quite simply. Prince Charles's investiture as Prince of Wales was arranged to take place in the summer of 1969 and, about eighteen months before this, applications began to pour into the Palace from television and film companies all over the world, all wanting facilities to make films about Prince Charles for showing at the time of his investiture. After a good deal of discussion – which all took place before I came on the scene – it was decided that it might be better to have one fully-backed film, made with the total cooperation of the Palace. Furthermore, instead of a film solely about Prince Charles, it should be mainly about the job he was one day going to have to do, and the only way to show that job was to film the work being done by the present Queen. So, for this special occasion, the Queen agreed that she would allow a film to be made showing the work of the monarch, including those aspects of the job which normally happen in private and which no one had seen before. It was in the spring of 1968 that I was approached and asked if I would make such a film.

I mention the date because the timing of this project was, as it happens, immensely important in relation to the state of documentary film-making. If it had happened four or five years earlier we would have made a very different sort of film. We could have shown the great state occasions and the more formal aspects of the monarch's job, but we could never have captured the informal moments as they actually happened. Above all, we would not have been able to convey to the audience the personalities of the Queen and her family, and in my view it was the revelation of these personalities, communicated directly into the homes of millions of people all over the world, that became the most important contribution the film was able to make.

In order to appreciate the importance of developments in documentary techniques in the mid-sixties, it is necessary to consider briefly what had happened before. Throughout the history of documentary film-making, in both television *and* cinema, one of the greatest problems (since the birth of talkies) had been the cumbersome nature of sound equipment. This was due mainly to the single fact that the intermittent motion of a film camera, jerking the celluloid through its gate, made so much noise that it would dominate the microphone if it were not suppressed in some way, and for thirty-five years the only effective way of doing this was to encase the camera in a vast, heavy sound-proof 'blimp'. To the documentary maker trying to capture the real world as naturally as possible, cumbersome equipment was an obvious handicap. Most producers took the easy

159. A monarch speaks – unseen – to his people: King George VI broadcasting to the nation from Buckingham Palace on the day of his coronation, 12 May 1937. Mass communication by the royal family earlier in this century was formal and restrained in style.

way out, and the great bulk of documentaries made for the cinema were shot silent, with a sound-track in the form of narration, background music and occasional sound effects added later. The people of the real world appeared on the screen, but they were rarely heard speaking.

It has often been said of film and television that visual images make the strongest impact, but the intelligence accompanying the images is conveyed, more often than not, by sound. It is *sound* which brings us, not merely facts, but the arguments, tensions, the hopes and fears, the personalities and the atmosphere of the real world. Although the first television documentaries inherited their form from the cinema, throughout the fifties and early sixties we had been attempting to use synchronised sound more and more on location. The cameras were still heavy and relatively immobile, so the sound sequences were mainly confined to set pieces – statements to camera by reporters, interviews, 'talking heads'. Documentary dialogue, such as it was, almost always had to be pre-arranged and rehearsed; spontaneity was virtually impossible. Even in 1963, when we were still using predominantly 35mm film in the BBC, it took two men to lift the sound camera onto its tripod.

The breakthrough came about in several ways. A number of straightforward but important developments reached fruition about that time. 16mm film equipment, previously the prerogative of the amateur, was finally perfected to demanding professional standards, so the size of cameras could be halved. With better film stock and lenses, artificial lighting could be reduced and sometimes dispensed with altogether. High-quality portable magnetic tape recorders, together with directional gun microphones, enabled a single-handed sound man to make excellent recordings several feet away from the person speaking. Above all, the so-called 'self-blimped' camera was invented: a camera which made *no* noise and was small enough for one man to operate from the shoulder. A two-man team could walk about, gathering perfect synchronised pictures and sound –

as they occurred and without preparation. People started talking about *cine-vérité* and hand-held photography, mistakenly believing that every wobble of the camera was responsible for the new naturalness, which was in fact coming from the spontaneity of the spoken word. By 1965 many documentary makers were filming *everything* with synchronised sound – even a passing bus. There continued to be – and there still is – a place for the conventional techniques, involving cameras on tripods and carefully-structured set-ups with scripts and prepared statements, but the hand-held techniques became essential for anything involving spontaneous action, natural dialogue and 'first-time' unrehearsed filming.

So when I was originally invited, in March 1968, to make an unprecedented documentary film about the job of the monarch and the role of the Queen and her family, my first reaction was that I needed the normal editorial freedom that I would expect in any film, and that I should be able to use the latest techniques, where appropriate, in order to include as much informality as possible. All this was agreed. Prince Philip formed a small advisory committee to help me with information and getting things done; at no point was I ever told how to make the film or what should be in it. Two key people on the committee were Lord Brabourne – John Brabourne, the film producer who had been involved with the original concept – and Bill Heseltine, at that time the Queen's Press Secretary, who was to become my vital link with the Palace during the year that followed, and whose acceptance and understanding of my film-making decisions was to help me more than anything else.

One of the ways in which this film differed from most was that it was about an unknown subject. No one, except members of the Palace household and the royal family themselves, had ever seen the day-to-day workings of the Palace. The spontaneous

Opposite: Princess Anne and Captain Mark Phillips shortly before their wedding in November 1973. Photograph by Norman Parkinson.

160
161

type of documentary does not, for obvious reasons, involve a detailed script, but the director is usually able to plan what he is going to do by studying his subject first. As I was about to film the Queen's work over a year, and as I only had fourteen months before the film was due to be transmitted, I had to do my research to some extent as I went along and let the film evolve in the process of shooting.

We started filming on 8 June 1968, with the scene of the Queen riding back after Trooping the Colour. Up to that moment, the Queen and Prince Philip were undoubtedly among the most photographed people in the world, but almost all the *filming* of them had been newsreel-type coverage of public events. The few exceptions were the very occasional 'facilities' when a group of selected photographers and newsreel men had been invited into the grounds of Sandringham or Buckingham Palace to take a few discreet shots of the Queen and her family. But on *no* occasion had microphones been allowed anywhere near, except for the making of formal and prepared speeches, and this is quite understandable when you consider that the Queen and Prince Philip are frequently surrounded by competing newsmen on the look-out for the scoop of an unguarded remark, and any words uttered are liable to be reported all over the world.

So, to begin with, the members of the royal family – and those close to them, including private detectives – found it very difficult to accept our microphones. But this type of filming depends on a process of familiarization. Whether you are filming a union dispute, or the Wilkins family of Reading, or soldiers on patrol in Belfast, or the men of the *Ark Royal*, the film crew must gradually cease to be strangers and must become familiar, accepted and ultimately trusted.

This was as true of *Royal Family* as of any other film, except that the process took rather longer than usual because of the exceptional circumstances.

Throughout the seventy-five days of filming – spread over a year – my crew never changed. Peter Bartlett, the cameraman, and Peter Edwards, the recordist, two of our younger technicians who had taken brilliantly to the new methods – gradually became so well known to the family and could work so close to them that, by September, we were able to do the scenes at Balmoral, including the picnic. After this necessary trust had developed, the project became a professional cooperation between the royal family, the director and the crew. Ultimately the Queen knew as well as anybody what the lighting set-up was, where the camera should be, how to avoid shadows, how to help the sound recordist.

I think the rest of the story is best told by the film itself. Two other key people were Michael Bradsell, who edited forty-three hours of material into one hundred and five minutes, and Antony Jay, who joined me as script consultant and who wrote the final commentary. But it was, as he and I agreed, essentially a 'how-it-works' commentary. by far the most important ingredient of the sound-track was the natural dialogue of the participants. And if it is true that *Royal Family* has been seen by more people throughout the world than any other documentary film, I believe that it is the personalities of those who appear in it that are responsible.

The documentary film *Royal Family* was made by a BBC/ITV consortium, by whom the photographs accompanying this article have been supplied.

Opposite
One of the most recent and most informal colour pictures of Queen Elizabeth II, taken on a visit to Silverwood Colliery, Yorkshire, 30 July 1975.

160. Buckingham Palace: the Queen 'in audience' with President Nyerere of Tanzania – the first time in history that part of an audience with a British sovereign had ever been photographed or filmed. The *cine-vérité* technique of the *Royal Family* team is shown by the close proximity of Peter Bartlett's wide-angle lens and Peter Edwards's microphone.

161. An early misty October morning on the Berkshire Downs.
One of the most beautifully photographed sequences in *Royal Family* showed the Queen studying the form of some of her race-horses with her trainer.

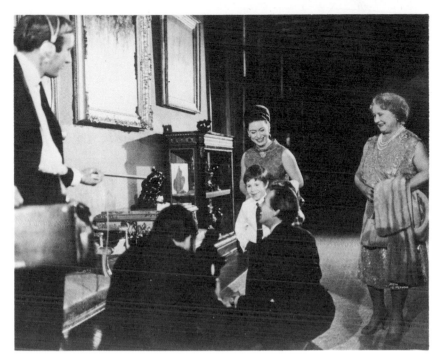

162. Christmas Eve at Windsor Castle, 1968. Lord Snowdon and Princess Margaret discuss the Gainsborough paintings on the wall with their seven-year-old son, Viscount Linley, while Queen Elizabeth, the Queen Mother, looks on.
The low camera angle demonstrates how hand-held equipment was used to capture informal situations as they developed.

163. After landing on the lawn at Buckingham Palace, Prince Philip hands over his Queen's Flight helicopter to its R.A.F. pilot, and to cameraman Peter Bartlett and director Richard Cawston for their low-level aerial filming over the Palace and the Mall.

164. At the end of a year of historic filming, the Queen poses with the B.B.C. crew who made *Royal Family*.
On the left of the Queen is Bill Heseltine, her Press Secretary at the time, and on the right, director/producer Richard Cawston.

165. Sandringham· Prince Edward, nearly five years old,
studies the Eclair camera with assistant cameraman Philip Bonham-Carter
shortly before being filmed in a snowball-fight with his brother Andrew.

80 years of royal films

This filmography (compiled October 1976) includes all identified silent films of British reigning monarchs in the National Film Archive. It also includes all sound documentary films held there, and a selection of the more important sound newsreels. Only films in which the reigning monarch appears are included.

SILENT FILMS

Queen Victoria 1837–1901

Oct 1896	Scenes at Balmoral – visit of their Imperial Majesties the Emperor and Empress of Russia to Balmoral J. & F. DOWNEY, South Shields
22.6.1897	Queen Victoria's Diamond Jubilee (numerous items)
also in	Royal Remembrances. Compilation, issued 1929; compiler Will Day GAUMONT
28.6.1897	The Queen's Garden Party at Buckingham Palace VELOGRAPH SYNDICATE
11.11.1899	Review of the Life Guards by H.M. the Queen WARWICK
c.1900	Queen Victoria leaves a military occasion BAMFORTH(?)
4.4.1900	The late Queen's visit to Dublin: royal procession entering the city gates, *in* Royal Remembrances, first film of a state visit HEPWORTH
1.2.1901	Funeral of Queen Victoria – numerous items showing the procession passing through London from Osborne House *en route* to Windsor HEPWORTH and others

Edward VII 1901–1910

1.2.1901	Funeral of Queen Victoria
May 1901	King Edward on the deck of his yacht WARWICK
16.1.1902	The King going to Parliament (State Opening) HEPWORTH
7.3.1902	. . . King Edward VII and Queen Alexandra visit Dartmouth to lay foundation stone of new Naval College HEPWORTH
25.6.1902	Coronation of Edward VII (numerous items) HEPWORTH, PAUL, WILLIAMSON and others
16.8.1902	The Naval Review after the Coronation HEPWORTH
25.10.1902	The King and Queen drive through the parts of London which had been omitted from the shortened coronation procession HEPWORTH and others
Feb 1903	State opening of Parliament by King Edward VII HEPWORTH
6.7.1903	The visit of President Loubet HEPWORTH
21–25.7.1903	King and Queen of England on a visit to Ireland HEPWORTH
20.2.1904	The King at Portsmouth
12.7.1904	King Edward VII opens Sheffield University SHEFFIELD PHOTO CO LTD
1906	Aberdeen University Quatercentenary Celebrations R. W. PAUL
10.2.1906	King Edward VII launches H.M.S. *Dreadnought* from Plymouth Dockyard URBAN
21.4.1906	Olympic Games at Athens
25.5.1907	Edward VII presenting medals to soldiers
9.7.1908	King Edward VII opens Royal Edward Dock at Avonmouth GAUMONT

Aug 1908	King Edward VII visits Bristol Art Gallery GAUMONT
Dec 1909	King Edward, though he has many mechanical vehicles, still prefers his horse . . . (also shows shooting party at Sandringham)
17.5.1910	Funeral of King Edward VII (numerous items) HEPWORTH, GAUMONT, WARWICK, WALTURDAW and others

George V 1910–1936

17.5.1910	Funeral of King Edward VII
c.1911	The King entertains 100,000 children CO-OPERATIVE CINEMATOGRAPH CO
1911	King's visit to the Middle East
6.2.1911	King George V opens his first Parliament in State PATHE, WARWICK
12.5.1911	Festival of Empire (various items of procession to Crystal Palace)
16.5.1911	Unveiling of the Queen Victoria Memorial in the Mall PATHE
29.5.1911	The King's second Levée at St James's Palace GAUMONT
31.5.1911	The Derby, 1911 GAUMONT, PATHE, WALTURDAW
22.6.1911	The Coronation of King George V (numerous items) URBAN, BARKER, PATHE, B & C, GAUMONT, HEPWORTH, JURY, CO-OP.
23.6.1911	King George V Royal Progress WARWICK, PATHE
29.6.1911	The Royal Progress to Guildhall HEPWORTH
1.7.1911	The King's Homecoming (return to Windsor) GAUMONT
10.7.1911	Royalty visit the Naval and Military Tournament at Olympia GAUMONT
13.7.1911	The Investiture of the Prince of Wales at Caernarvon (various items) GAUMONT, PATHE, URBAN, HEPWORTH
15.7.1911	The King and Queen at the laying of the foundation stone of the National Library of Wales at Aberystwyth PATHE
17.7.1911	Royal Visit to Scotland: Edinburgh welcomes the King and Queen
19.7.1911	The King and Queen at the laying of the Memorial Stone of the Usher Hall, Edinburgh PATHE
12.12.1911	King George V's Coronation Durbar at Delhi (various items) PATHE, WARWICK, BARKER
c.1912	Military Parade
1912	The King and Queen amongst the troops (probably at Aldershot) PATHE
5.2.1912	The return of the King and Queen from the state visit to India: arrival at Portsmouth GAUMONT
7.5.1912	His Majesty landing at Weymouth
11.5.1912	King comes ashore at Weymouth to receive address from civic officials PATHE

c.1913	Their Majesties' busy Whitsuntide		20.7.1914	The King, on board the royal yacht *Victoria & Albert*, leads the Fleet to sea TOPICAL BUDGET
c.1913–15	Their Majesties at Aldershot 'War'		8.9.1914	The King and Queen visit our wounded soldiers at King's College Hospital WARWICK
1913(?)	Opening of Parliament			
6.3.1913	The King enjoys Army & Navy match at Queens Club GAUMONT		12.11.1914	The State Opening of Parliament TOPICAL BUDGET
22.4.1913	England – the King and Queen amongst the workers: Their Majesties visit the Five Towns: the Mayor and Corporation receive them at Newcastle-under-Lyme WARWICK		1914–15	His Majesty at the Front: King George has gone to France to visit the 'Contemptible Little Army' PATHE
			c.1–5 Dec	
			11.2.1915	The King inspects the third convoy of motor ambulances organised by the British Ambulance Committee GAUMONT
19.5.1913	The Royal visit to Germany: Their Majesties' arrival in Berlin GAUMONT			
24.5.1913	The German royal wedding GAUMONT		11.2.1915	The King inspects troops: His Majesty reviews Kitchener's Army at Cambridge PATHE
27.5.1913	King George V and the Emperor William attend great military display at Potsdam, at the end of the King's visit to Germany GAUMONT		22.3.1915	H.M. the King reviews 2,000 members of the City of London National Guard at Buckingham Palace TOPICAL BUDGET
13.6.1913	King and Queen attend the Chapter of the Order of the Garter at Windsor PATHE		21.8.1915	Royal visit to the Royal Pavilion Hospital, Brighton
			5.6.1916	Massed bands at the Albert Hall GAUMONT
16.6.1913	King George V visits Eton School PATHE		6.6.1916	H.M. the King reviews troops ECLAIR
4.7.1913	Royalty busy . . . Bristol Show . . . PATHE		c.1917	Prince of Wales with King George V and Queen Mary at the quayside GAUMONT
c.6.7.1913	His Majesty reviews his citizen troops in Hyde Park PATHE			
7–11.7.1913	King and Queen's visit to Yorks and Lancs		12.2.1917	The King opens Parliament GAUMONT
7–11.7.1913	The King reviews two London Divisions of the Territorial Force in Hyde Park PATHE		26.2.1917	King George in the City: opens new School of Oriental Studies GAUMONT
9.7.1913	The visit of the King and Queen Mary to Colne		4.6.1917	Decorating nurses: nurses receiving the Royal Red Cross from the King TOPICAL BUDGET
11.7.1913	King George V and Queen Mary visit Liverpool			
29.7–1.8.1913	The King at Goodwood Races PATHE		18.6.1917	The King visits Tyneside TOPICAL BUDGET
23.9.1913	The King is presented with a civic address at Northampton PATHE		5.7.1917	Canadian Commemoration: Their Majesties attend solemn service at Westminster Abbey GAUMONT
1914–18	King George and Queen Mary embark on a ship		2.8.1917	His Majesty invests war heroes at Buckingham Palace GAUMONT
1914–18	King George V and Queen Mary at a railway station			
1914–18	King George V and Queen Mary inspect Allied troops		15.8.1917	London welcomes the American Troops: . reviewed by H.M. the King after marching past the American Embassy PATHE
1914–18	The King in khaki			
c.1914–15	Royal visit to a county town		16.8.1917	At the Palace: . American officers presented to the King TOPICAL BUDGET
12.2.1914	King George opens his fourth Parliament GAUMONT			
23.4.1914	Paris en Fête: special races held at Auteuil in honour of the King and Queen PATHE		1.10.1917	Queen Mary among the tanks TOPICAL BUDGET
			12.2.1918	H.M. the King opens Parliament in State GAUMONT GRAPHIC
23.4.1914	Royal visit to Paris: the King and Queen received with military honours at Calais GAUMONT			
30.4.1914	The King visits Leys School, Cambridge PATHE		14.3.1918	The King and Queen at Reading TOPICAL BUDGET
22.6.1914	Trooping the Colour TOPICAL BUDGET		18.3.1918	Reading honoured. King and Queen visit the 'biscuit' town GAUMONT
24.6.1914	Royal Midlands Tour: 20,000 children give three cheers at Nottingham PATHE			
			2.5.1918	The Mole Men: King and Queen's visit to the heroic Zeebrugge survivors TOPICAL BUDGET
25.6.1914	Visit of the King and Queen to Nottingham TOPICAL BUDGET			
			9.5.1918	Strenuous Canadian fighters: the King and Sir Edward Kemp (High Commissioner) witness keen training TOPICAL BUDGET
26.6.1914	Royal Hull visit: Their Majesties arrive at the City Hall PATHE			
27.6.1914	The King and Queen review the London Fire Brigade in Hyde Park (various items) PATHE, TOPICAL BUDGET, GAUMONT		14.5.1918	. . . Historic march past of U.S. soldiers of the Second 5,000 from Wellington Barracks . . . TOPICAL BUDGET
			23.5.1918	His Majesty visits Inter-Allied Exhibition at Central Hall, Westminster GAUMONT
29.6.1914	The King opens King George V Dock at Hull GAUMONT			
29.6.1914	Nottingham children welcome the King and Queen GAUMONT		25.5.1918	Nurses honoured by the King: members of Queen Alexandra's Imperial Service receive Royal Red Cross at Buckingham Palace TOPICAL BUDGET
3.7.1914	The King and Agriculture: His Majesty talks to veteran agriculturalists and watches dairymaids at the Shrewsbury Royal Show PATHE		27.5.1918	Open-air Investiture at Buckingham Palace TOPICAL BUDGET
			27.5.1918	King and Queen at Stirling Works (Essex?) GAUMONT
6.7.1914	The King visits the Royal Agricultural Show at Shrewsbury TOPICAL BUDGET		27.5.1918	Their Majesties visit Telephone and Fuse Factory in Essex GAUMONT
8.7.1914	Royal Scottish tour: Glasgow's reception of the King and Queen PATHE		30.5.1918	Their Majesties at Albert Hall (Empire Day Celebrations) GAUMONT
9.7.1914	The King and Queen board the battleship *Benbow* in construction at Dalmuir on the Clyde TOPICAL BUDGET		6.6.1918	King and Queen at Leeds GAUMONT
			26.6.1918	A 'Master Cutter': Their Majesties visit Army Clothing Department; King cuts out 50 suits GAUMONT
18.7.1914	Naval Review, 1914 BARKER		4.7.1918	Silver Wedding Pageant GAUMONT

8.7.1918	Independence Day: Their Majesties at American baseball match at Chelsea GAUMONT
23.7.1918	Official film: recording historic incidents in His Majesty's visit to the Grand Fleet
25.7.1918	King and Queen at South West London allotments GAUMONT
8.8.1918	Remembrance Day: Their Majesties attend service at Westminster Abbey GAUMONT
21.10 1918	King and Queen at American Hospital, Dartford GAUMONT
c.11.1918	King George V with his ministers
18.11.1918	Free Churches Thanksgiving: King and Queen attend service at Albert Hall TOPICAL BUDGET
c.21.11.1918	The Surrender of the German Navy GAUMONT
21.11.1918	King aboard (battleship) Queen Elizabeth TOPICAL BUDGET
9.12.1918	King, Prince of Wales, Prince Albert, in Paris GAUMONT
1919	The Victory Leaders. director: Maurice Elvey (documentary) STOLL FILM CO
1919	London and its Life (documentary) KINETO
30.6.1919	How London received the news (of the Armistice): great patriotic demonstration to the royal family at Buckingham Palace TOPICAL BUDGET
30.6.1919	Lloyd George back from Paris: King greets Premier at Victoria Station and conducts him to Buckingham Palace TOPICAL BUDGET
31.7.1919	Their Majesties receive Peace Address at Guildhall GAUMONT
c.1920	H.M. the King at Chiswick – opens new Civil Service Sports Ground
10.2.1920	Royal Drive TOPICAL BUDGET
11.10.1920	The Ambassador of Empire: Prince of Wales has now completed his tour of the Dominions: . . . welcome home . . . GAUMONT
6.12.1920	Royalty at the Advertising Exhibition (White City) GAUMONT
12.12.1920	King George V with 70,000 football crowd TOPICAL BUDGET
10.2.1921	King and Queen at notable wedding: Hon Alexander Hardinge . . . married to Helen, daughter of Lord Edward Cecil, at St Paul's, Knightsbridge TOPICAL BUDGET
23.6.1921	King opens Northern Ireland Parliament at Belfast GAUMONT
6.6.1921	London's new bridge across the Thames: H.M. the King, accompanied by the Queen, opens new Southwark Bridge
11.7.1921	London's new dock opened by H.M. the King for Port of London Authority GAUMONT
6.12.1921	Peace Council at the Palace TOPICAL BUDGET
c.1922	King and Queen at opening of the championships TOPICAL BUDGET
1922	Through Three Reigns (documentary; compilation of events from 1896 to 1911) HEPWORTH
2.3.1922	Wedding of Princess Mary to Viscount Lascelles (various items) TOPICAL BUDGET, GAUMONT
5.6.1922	Trooping the Colour GAUMONT
15.6.1922	Richmond Royal Horse Show GAUMONT
20.7.1922	New London County Hall opened by the King GAUMONT
21.7.1922	12,000 royal guests. Bird's-eye view from the Vernon Court Hotel of their Majesties' Garden Party at Buckingham Palace TOPICAL BUDGET
19.8.1922	Ballater: King's holiday in the Highlands PATHE
12.10.1922	Royal visit to Edinburgh GAUMONT
23.11.1922	London: State Opening of Parliament PATHE, GAUMONT
14.12.1922	Oxford v Cambridge at Twickenham GAUMONT
13.2.1923	State Opening of Parliament GAUMONT GRAPHIC
26.4.1923	H.R.H. The Duke of York – married at Westminster Abbey to Elizabeth Bowes-Lyon (various items) GAUMONT, PATHE, TOPICAL BUDGET
9.5.1923	Royal visit to Italy GAUMONT
14.5.1923	Their Majesties at the Vatican: visit of King and Queen to the Pope GAUMONT
17.5.1923	The King in Italy: attends horse show at the Villa Borghese GAUMONT
4.6.1923	New Nurses' home – Their Majesties lay foundation stone at University College Hospital
11.6.1923	The King and Queen at Stratford GAUMONT
21.6.1923	Royal Ascot
10.7.1923	Their Majesties in Scotland GAUMONT
28.7.1923	The King and Queen in South London – great reception in Wandsworth GAUMONT
13.12.1923	H.M. the King sees Cambridge defeated . . . by Oxford's unbeaten XV GAUMONT
27.12.1923	Looking back: the Gaumont Graphic presents a review of some of the principal events of 1923 GAUMONT
17.1.1924	State Opening of Parliament GAUMONT
23.4.1924	King opens Empire Exhibition TOPICAL BUDGET
12.5.1924	Romania's King and Queen: state reception on first official royal visit since pre-war GAUMONT
14.5.1924	Monarch's Tour of the British Empire: King and Queen escort Ferdinand and Queen Marie through Britain's Dominions at Wembley TOPICAL BUDGET
2.6.1924	Honouring Wembley: visit to Exhibition with royal Italian guests GAUMONT
26.7.1924	The King with his Fleet (at Spithead) TOPICAL BUDGET
7.8.1924	The King at Cowes GAUMONT
9.12.1924	Parliament opened in State TOPICAL BUDGET, GAUMONT
20.12.1924	England wins the Calcutta Cup GAUMONT
1925	January – 'Topical' Review of 1924 TOPICAL BUDGET
16.2.1925	Investiture GAUMONT
4.6.1925	His Majesty's 60th Birthday: Trooping the Colour GAUMONT
8.6.1925	King George V and Queen Mary visit Bristol TOPICAL BUDGET
28.6.1925	Their Majesties . . . with the Duke and Duchess of York, inspecting the Vickers Vanguard
2.7.1925	Wonderful airmanship at Hendon: the royal family witness thrilling evolution in the air at R.A.F. Pageant GAUMONT
2.7.1925	H.M. the King opens Dominions new H.Q. in London
20.7.1925	Royal Party at Sandown Park GAUMONT
23.7.1925	H.M. the King opens Kenwood, Hampstead GAUMONT
30.7.1925	The charm of Goodwood GAUMONT
10.9.1925	The King at Braemar – greatest of all Highland gatherings TOPICAL BUDGET
11.11.1925	Remembrance Day TOPICAL BUDGET
c.20.11.1925	Queen Alexandra: It is with profound regret that 'Topical Budget' records the death of the Queen Mother at Sandringham (various items) TOPICAL BUDGET
18.2.1926	The King and Queen at White City – British Industries Fair GAUMONT
11.4.1926	King and Royal Engineers. His Majesty's visit of inspection at Chatham TOPICAL BUDGET

16.4.1926	An English home, in Royal Remembrances
15–18.6.1926	Royal Ascot: Their Majesties greeted by 'King Sol' TOPICAL BUDGET
3.7.1926	Ascot of the Air (Hendon) TOPICAL BUDGET
22.7.1926	12,000 guests entertained by their Majesties at Buckingham Palace TOPICAL BUDGET
26.8.1926	The King in Scotland: the arrival of His Majesty at Ballater en route for Balmoral GAUMONT
c.1927	King Faud's welcome TOPICAL BUDGET
21.4.1927	Wales: Royal Visit to Cardiff TOPICAL BUDGET
16.5.1927	. . . The French President's triumphal entry into London as the King's guest TOPICAL BUDGET
25.6.1927	. . . The Household Cavalry receive new Standards from H.M. the King GAUMONT, TOPICAL BUDGET
27.6.1927	The homecoming of the Duke and Duchess of York TOPICAL BUDGET
12.7.1927	Royal visit to Glasgow PATHE
1928	Twenty Years Ago. Satire of topical pictures 1896–1928 editor: Ben R. Hart BRITISH SCREEN CLASSICS
24.3.1928	An International Institution: The King . . . opens new Lloyds, of which he laid the foundation stone 3 years ago TOPICAL BUDGET
21.3.1928	Their Majesties visit Aldershot and inspect Army Vocational Training Centre TOPICAL BUDGET
15–16.6.1928	The King with his cavalry GAUMONT
18–19.6.1928	Scintillating Ascot GAUMONT
3.6.1929	Military pageant of scarlet and gold . . . Trooping the Colour EMPIRE NEWS BULLETIN
1.7.1929	. . . Vast crowds give H.M. the King a tumultuous welcome on his return to Buckingham Palace after nearly 5 months' absence (various items) PATHE, EMPIRE NEWS BULLETIN
7.7.1929	Westminster Abbey. His Majesty leads the Empire in thanksgiving for his recovery BRITISH SCREEN NEWS
c.1930	Air Force review with King George V GAUMONT
c.1930	Ballater – the King in Scotland PATHE
c.1930	The State Opening of Parliament PATHE
Jan 1930	Tempus Fugit 1929–30 (review of the year) EMPIRE NEWS BULLETIN
26.4.1930	King George V and Duke of York at Wembley Cup Final
25.6.1930	King George V leaving St Paul's with Queen Mary
21.8.1930	A daughter for the 'Dainty Duchess': the whole nation acclaims the birth of a new Princess at Glamis PATHE
11.11.1930	King George V at Cenotaph with Prince of Wales and Duke of York
1931	21st Anniversary: 1910–1931 (review) PATHE
1931	Look back on 1930 PATHE
28.5.1931	King and Queen open Royal Tournament BRITISH SCREEN NEWS
18.7.1931	Their Majesties at Ilford BRITISH SCREEN NEWS
24.4.1932	Arsenal v Newcastle, Cup Final 1932 GAUMONT
26.7.1933	Largest Dry Dock: King inaugurates new graving dock at Southampton UNIVERSAL NEWS

SOUND FILMS

25.12.1934	King's Christmas Speech, 1934
1935	Jubilee (documentary contrasting the 1935 Jubilee celebrations with working class poverty) NORTH LONDON FILM SOCIETY
1935	The King's Jubilee (review of royal occasions from 1896 to King's radio message to the Empire) GAUMONT BRITISH FILMS
1935	Royal Cavalcade (compilation of newsreel and reconstruction material issued for Jubilee of George V) BRITISH INTERNATIONAL PICTURES
1936	In Memoriam George V, 1910–1936 UNIVERSAL NEWS
20.1.1936	In Memoriam King George V (various items) BRITISH MOVIETONE, PATHE, GAUMONT
24–28.1.1936	Lying in State at Westminster Hall (various items) BRITISH MOVIETONE
28.1.1936	Funeral of King George V PARAMOUNT, UNIVERSAL
1948	The Peaceful Years, 1920–1936 PATHE DOCUMENTARY UNIT

Edward VIII (Duke of Windsor) 1936

22.1.1936	Proclamation of King Edward VIII GAUMONT
15.5.1936	King Edward VIII inspecting Troops PATHE GAZETTE
3–11.12.1936	The King Abdicates (various items) BRITISH MOVIETONE, PARAMOUNT, PATHE, UNIVERSAL

George VI 1936–1952

11.12.1936	The Royal Family
12.12.1936	Proclamation [of the Abdication and the Accession of George VI] (various items) BRITISH MOVIETONE, PATHE
1937	Crown and Glory (documentary – story of the British Empire from 1858 to proclamation of George VI) PARAMOUNT
17.3.1937	King visits tenants of the Duchy of Cornwall estates in East London BRITISH MOVIETONE
29.3.1937	George VI: a retrospect of the King's life BRITISH MOVIETONE
23.4.1937	Remembrance: His Majesty unveils Windsor Memorial to George V BRITISH MOVIETONE
26.4.1937	Royalty: the King, the Queen, the Princesses BRITISH MOVIETONE
29.4.1937	The King: His Majesty reviews Scouts and goes by river to Greenwich BRITISH MOVIETONE
12.5.1937	The Coronation of George VI (various items) MOVIETONE, PATHE, GAUMONT, UNIVERSAL
19–21.5.1937	Coronation: the Naval Review (various items) MOVIETONE
9.6.1937	Trooping the Colour (in colour) BRITISH MOVIETONE
14.6.1937	Their Majesties attend Garter Service at Windsor BRITISH MOVIETONE
22.6.1937	Their Majesties hold first Garden Party of the reign BRITISH MOVIETONE
3.7.1937	The King and Queen attend first Great Festival of Youth at Wembley BRITISH MOVIETONE
c.5.7.1937	Royal Visit to Scotland, 1937 (various items) GAUMONT
6.7.1937	King George VI opens the Empire Exhibition at Bellahouston Park, Glasgow BRITISH MOVIETONE
19–22.7.1938	Royal Visit to France MOVIETONE
6.5–26.6.1939	Royal Tour of Canada (various items) and the U.S.A. BRITISH MOVIETONE, GAUMONT
1939	The Royal Visit (short documentary) CANADIAN GOVT MOTION PICTURE BUREAU
4–10.12.1939	Visit of George VI to B.E.F. (Western Front) JOURNAL DE GUERRE
1940	Royal Review (documentary of royal events from 1937 to 1939) PARAMOUNT
20.6.1940	Royalty visit the wounded BRITISH NEWS
17.7.1940	King visits ANZACs in camp BRITISH NEWS

14.8.1940	King visits Indian Army camp in Derbyshire BRITISH NEWS
11–16.9.1940	King and Queen inspect bomb damage at Buckingham Palace, and visit bombed areas in South East London BRITISH NEWS
29.12.1940	King and Queen Elizabeth visit South Wales BRITISH NEWS
30.4.1942	King and Queen review Canadian Armoured Division in England BRITISH PARAMOUNT NEWS
3–4.6.1942	King and Queen in Scotland: visit Clydeside and Edinburgh GAUMONT BRITISH
28.6.1943	The King's visit to North Africa BRITISH NEWS
12.7.1943	The King confers with Allied commanders BRITISH NEWS
29.5.1944	His Majesty visits Home Fleet BRITISH NEWS
14.8.1944	The King in Italy BRITISH NEWS
30.10.1944	The King visits the Western Front BRITISH NEWS
22.1.1945	The Royal Family at Windsor BRITISH NEWS
16.4.1945	President Roosevelt receives the King and Queen (compilation in memorial to Roosevelt) BRITISH MOVIETONE
3.12.1945	Review of Victory Year GAUMONT BRITISH
10.6.1946	Royal Family at Windsor Horse Show BRITISH NEWS
c.30.6.1946	Continuing the Royal Tour of Scotland BRITISH MOVIETONE
26.10.1946	Royal Family at Mountbatten Wedding BRITISH MOVIETONE
10.11.1946	In Remembrance of Two Wars: Remembrance Day service at the Cenotaph BRITISH MOVIETONE
11.11.1946	The Royal Command Film Performance (A Matter of Life and Death) BRITISH NEWS
1947	The Royal Tour of South Africa (documentary on the tour)
3.2.1947	The Royal Tour – departure for South Africa (numerous items on all stages of the tour) BRITISH MOVIETONE
19.5.1947	Royal Welcome Home BRITISH NEWS
14.7.1947	Royal visit to Wimbledon BRITISH NEWS
16.10.1947	The Royal Family: new pictures BRITISH MOVIETONE
22.10.1947	Unveiling of King George V statue BRITISH MOVIETONE
20.11.1947	The Royal Wedding (Princess Elizabeth and Duke of Edinburgh)
11.3.1948	Royal visitors at Ideal Home Exhibition BRITISH MOVIETONE
26.4.1948	Royal Silver Wedding BRITISH MOVIETONE
12.4.1948	Roosevelt Memorial unveiled BBC
19.7.1948	His Majesty at Sandhurst 'Passing Out' parade BRITISH MOVIETONE
22.7.1948	Shah of Persia visits England BRITISH MOVIETONE
18.10.1948	His Majesty meets Commonwealth Premiers BRITISH MOVIETONE
7.11.1948	Remembrance Day (last appearance of George VI at this ceremony) BRITISH MOVIETONE
25.11.1948	His Majesty the King (shows the King's failing health) BRITISH MOVIETONE
15.12.1948	Royal Prince christened (Prince Charles) BRITISH MOVIETONE
20.10.1950	Christening of Princess Anne BBC
1951	Fifty Royal Years (compilation of events from 1897 to christening of Princess Anne) GAUMONT BRITISH
7.5.1951	The Festival of Britain (opening ceremony and royal tour) BRITISH MOVIETONE
8.5.1951	State visit of the King and Queen of Denmark GAUMONT BRITISH
12.5.1951	King with British Legion MOVIETONE

Elizabeth II 1952–

1952	The King Who Loved His Family (compilation on the life of King George VI) PATHE DOCUMENTARY UNIT
1952	Queen Elizabeth II: an appreciation MOVIETONE
15.2.1952	Tribute to King George VI (various items) BRITISH MOVIETONE
8.6.1952	Trooping the Colour MOVIETONE
19.6.1952	Royal Ascot UNIVERSAL
9.7.1952	The Queen's Investiture MOVIETONE
7.8.1952	Royal Family in Scotland PATHE
4.11.1952	Queen opens Parliament PATHE
9.11.1952	Queen pays homage (Cenotaph service) PATHE
14–16.4.1953	Royal Diary PATHE
23.6.1953	The Coronation of Queen Elizabeth II GAUMONT
1953	A Queen is Crowned (colour documentary on the Coronation) RANK
1953	Royal Review (3-D documentary short) A.B. PATHE
1953	Gentlemen – The Queen (documentary short) GAUMONT BRITISH
1953	Long to Reign Over Us (record of the reign of George VI and Accession of Queen Elizabeth)
11.6.1953	Trooping the Colour
15.7.1953	Coronation Fly-Past PATHE
23.11.1953	Queen leaves on World Tour GAUMONT
1954	The Queen in Australia (official film of the Royal Tour) AUSTRALIAN NATIONAL FILM BOARD
1954	Royal Visit to Bermuda (documentary) BERMUDA TRAVEL DEVELOPMENT BOARD
15.6.1954	Ceremony of the Garter (installation of Winston Churchill) BBC
21.10.1955	In Commemoration – Queen unveils statue of George VI at Westminster MOVIETONE
1956	Welcome to the Queen (record of the visit of the Queen and Duke to Teesside, June 1956. Colour)
23.3.1956	Coventry Cathedral – Queen lays foundation stone PATHE
16.7.1956	State visit of King Faisal of Iraq BBC
18.4.1957	St Alban's – the Royal Maundy PATHE
4.6.1957	Queen's flight by Comet GAUMONT BRITISH
25.12.1957	The Queen's Christmas Message (first TV transmission) BBC
1957	The Sceptre and the Mace (constitutional history of England, on occasion of royal visit to Canada) NATIONAL FILM BOARD OF CANADA
13.5.1958	The Queen greets Italy's President GAUMONT BRITISH
9.6.1958	Queen opens Gatwick (Airport) PATHE
5.12.1958	Bristol: Queen dials Edinburgh (STD inaugurated) PATHE
17.2.1959	Badminton Trials BRITISH MOVIETONE
29.4.1959	Queen and Prince Charles visits H.M.S. Eagle TELEVISION ROTA SERVICE (TRS)
29.6–24.7.1959	Queen and Duke of Edinburgh tour Canada TRS
29.8.1959	Eisenhower with Royal Family at Balmoral TRS
11.9.1959	The Shah's visit PATHE
21.10.1959	The Queen in U.S.A. PATHE
2.2.1960	The Royal Baby (Prince Andrew) PATHE
5.4.1960	Arrival of President de Gaulle at Buckingham Palace (various items)
6.5.1960	Princess Margaret's Wedding (various items)
6.7.1960	Queen opens Flamstead House TRS
19.7.1960	Royal Society Tercentenary TRS
5.8.1960	Queen and Duke of Edinburgh attend Eisteddfod at Cardiff TRS

1961	Queen Elizabeth II in Pakistan (documentary) CENTRAL OFFICE OF INFORMATION
Jan – March 1961	Royal Tour of India (various items on all stages of the tour)
14.8.1961	Queen visits Northern Ireland PATHE
2.11.1961	Queen at BBC TV Centre TRS
20.11.1961	Queen in North Ghana PATHE
30.11.1961	Queen in Sierra Leone PATHE
29.10.1962	Queen and Duke at the Royal Variety Show TRS
18.2.1963	Royal Progress in New Zealand PATHE
4.3.1963	The Queen Down Under (Australia) PATHE
10.6.1964	Queen and Duke of Edinburgh at service to commemorate 750th anniversary of Magna Carta TRS
23.7.1964	Queen and King Hussein at Royal Tournament TRS
8.2.1965	Royal Visit to Africa PATHE
11.2.1965	Tour of Triumph – Ethiopia (colour) PATHE
20.5.1965	The Queen in Germany PATHE

17.5.1966	The Queen opens new G.P.O. Tower TRS
10.1966	Queen and Duke of Edinburgh visit Aberfan TRS
24.4.1968	Queen's 42nd Birthday PATHE
17.11.1968	Royal Tour of South America (various items) PATHE
1969	The Royal Family (colour documentary; director: Richard Cawston) BBC/ITV
11.5.1969	State visit to Austria PATHE
25.5.1969	Queen attends General Assembly of Church of Scotland PATHE
3.7.1969	Investiture at Caernarvon of the Prince of Wales (various items)
7–12.8.1969	Royal Family visiting Norway PATHE
12.10.1973	Queen's visit to Canada (various items)
14.11.1973	Wedding of H.R.H. Princess Anne to Captain Mark Phillips BRITISH MOVIETONE
1974	Opening of the Sydney Opera House by the Queen (official film; documentary)

166. The formidably cumbersome equipment necessary before the technical advances of the mid-sixties is indicated in this photograph of the film crew of *Elizabeth is Queen*, the Associated British Pathé production released in June 1953.

167. Fan decorated with photographs of members of the royal
families of Great Britain and Europe, *c*.1895. In their
enthusiasm for photography, the Victorians devised some
ingenious and often surprising uses for this new and exciting
technique. Photo mezzotype printed by the London
Stereoscopic Company.

133

Acknowledgements

The following photographs are reproduced by
gracious permission of Her Majesty The Queen: 7, 8, 9, 10, 18, 21, 22, 23, 24, 25, 27, 32, 33, 49, 50, 51, 52, 53,
61, 62, 66, 67, 73, 80, 81, 82, 83, 84, 85, 86, 87, 88, 90, 91, 92, 93, 94, 95, 96, 97, 98, 99, 100,
101, 102, 103, 104, 105, 106, 107, 108, 109, 115, 116, 117, 119, 121, 126,
colour plates page 49, page 50 (memorial ring), page 68

Aberdeen Public Libraries: 56, 69, 71, 74 front cover (Queen Victoria)

Sir Michael Balcon: colour plate page 67

Sir Cecil Beaton: 6, 130, 131, 132, 133, 134, 135

British Broadcasting Corporation: 159

British Broadcasting Corporation/Independent Television Consortium: 160, 161, 162, 163, 164, 165

British Newspaper Library: 26

Camera Club: 127, 128, 129

Camera Press: colour plate page 101, front cover (Queen Elizabeth II)

Central Press Photos: 144, 151, 152

Fox Photos: 150

John Hillelson Agency: 139, 140

Howarth-Loomes Collection: 167

Keystone Press Agency: 138, 146

Kodak Museum: 89

Patrick Lichfield: 20, colour plate page 102, back cover

Manchester Evening News: 17

National Coal Board: colour plate page 120

National Film Archive: 30, 31, 149, 158, 166

National Portrait Gallery:
1, 3, 4, 5, 11, 12, 13, 14, 15, 16, 19, 28, 29, 37, 38, 39, 40, 41, 42, 43, 44, 45, 46, 47, 48, 54, 58,
64, 65, 76, 77, 78, 79, 110, 111, 112, 113, 114, 118, 120, 122, 123, 124, 125, 136, 137, 141, 142, 143, 145,
148, 153, 155, 156, 157, colour plate page 50 (cartes-de-visite)

Norman Parkinson: colour plate page 119

Popperfoto: 2, 147, 154

Private collections: 34, 35, 36, 55, 57, 59, 60, 63, 68, 70, 72, 75

Punch Publications Ltd: cartoon on page 136

Index

Page numbers in bold type refer to illustrations

Cartoon by Rupert Besley,
from *Punch*, 23 June 1976.